The Gospel in
Philippians

Displaying God in godless times

Contributors

Carlos Astorga, Th.M.
Rhome van Dyck, Th.M.
S. Jonathan Murphy, Ph.D.
Vanessa van Dyck, M.Ed., M.A.[BS]

Field Notes

a journal of exploration and discovery

SacraScript

The Gospel in Philippians:
Displaying God in godless times

Field Notes
Copyright © 2013 Sacra Script Ministries

Published by:
Sacra Script Ministries
2001 West Plano Parkway, Suite 1010, Plano, TX 75075
www.SacraScript.org

Printed in the United States of America

0413.1

For comments, corrections or suggestions, email us at
comments@SacraScript.org

Find us on Facebook at www.facebook.com/SacraScriptMinistries
or Twitter at www.twitter.com/sacrascript

The Purpose of Sacra Script

In the book of Acts chapter 8, Philip was prompted by the Holy Spirit to catch up with an Ethiopian eunuch reading from Isaiah 53 in his chariot. Philip asked the eunuch if he understood what he was reading. The eunuch replied, "How could I unless someone explains it to me?" The experience of the eunuch is common to most people. Just like Philip, Sacra Script's goal is to explain Scripture in light of the Lord Jesus Christ.

The Sacra Script creative team includes gifted pastor-teachers and biblical educators. We seek to explain the Bible within the context in which it was written and help you learn the necessary skills for application. We have also designed exercises and study questions to help you remember and respond to what you have learned so that your Bible study does not end at information but transformation. We have carefully included many different tools to help you understand God's Word. These *Field Notes* include detailed written explanations, outlines, word studies, pictures, notes, illustrations, maps, and timelines in order to capture the meaning of the text in its ancient context. As a result, this book is part guide, part atlas, part Bible dictionary, part history, and part student workbook.

Whether you have never opened the Bible or are seasoned in the faith, these *Field Notes* provide integrated learning of the Bible. Our resources also include an *Expedition Guide* for pastors, teachers, and facilitators which utilize additional notes, references, and teaching aids. Video and audio versions designed to better engage visual and auditory learners are also available. Lastly, a digital version guides the student through the biblical text online or through a variety of media technologies.

At Sacra Script our prayer is that through the study of God's Word and the aid of the Holy Spirit you would come to comprehend and apply the Bible. God gave us his word so that we can understand his will. He wants us to be informed about, and involved in, his plan for the ages. This plan for the ages is a gospel plan; it is good news. The gospel is that eternal life with God is made available by God. It is offered only through the Son of God, Jesus Christ, whose death and resurrection alone satisfies God's wrath toward sin. You can receive God's forgiveness and be assured of eternal life by trusting in Jesus Christ. This is good news. This is the gospel, and all of Scripture points to it.

for more information visit
www.SacraScript.org

This book is a testimony to God's faithfulness
working through his people. Without our team
of supporters giving to the work of the Lord,
this book would not have been written.
May God use these words to build and edify his Church
for the glory of our LORD and Savior Jesus Christ.

Table of Contents

IV. Analyze the Find

V. Toolbox

How does this book work?
Field Notes

Keys to your Field Notes

Welcome to your *Field Notes* on Philippians. You are about to embark on a journey of discovery. Your destination is Christianity in the regions of Rome and Philippi in the first century A.D. In order to be ready for your exploration of this book, we highly recommend you spend a few minutes understanding the way your *Field Notes* work. This book serves as a guide to the ancient biblical text as well as a journal for your discoveries along the way. Let's get started.

Studying the Bible
Studying the Bible is much like heading off into an unknown land to dig around the ruins of an ancient civilization. You need to know where to dig, what you are discovering, and what is important about what you find. This book will guide you on a journey of ancient discovery: the discovery of the meaning of the biblical text.

This Bible study follows the metaphor of an expedition, or a quest in search of biblical and theological discovery. Your *Field Notes* contain three specific parts which correspond to the three steps used in an ancient dig. Each step will help you in the process of understanding and applying God's Word to your life. Each *Field Study* begins with learning the content and meaning of the text, followed by a section called *Discoveries,* which includes discussion questions, exercises, and activities to apply the text to your life. Let's begin by understanding the three steps.

Step one: Survey the land
The first step to making a discovery is a comprehensive survey of the land, noting everything that is around. In your *Field Notes*, the site is the biblical book we will study. This inspection helps us to better understand the characteristics of the terrain. With regard to the Bible, our survey helps us see the function of a book as part of the grand

A Field Study

Your *Field Notes* are divided into individual field studies. Each *Field Study* is designed to take a minimum of 30 minutes. The content of the *Field Study* takes around fifteen minutes to read, and the remaining time is for the *Discoveries*. This includes discussion questions, exercises, and activities which provide over an hour's worth of interaction if so desired. The exercises are designed for you to choose the ones that are most helpful for you or your group.

story of Scripture. We see all the general aspects that provide us the information we need to appreciate the significance of the text once we start our excavation.

Our survey requires the right tools: a compass to know in what direction we are going and a map to understand the lay of the land. Our biblical survey will explore issues related to the historical background of the book, date of composition, author, and intended audience. We will also learn the significance of the book in the Bible, its literary style, and the necessary information for a detailed understanding. Essentially, we will learn all we can to understand what the original audience already knew when they received the writing. This way, as we read the biblical text, we will be closer to thinking the same thoughts as the original audience, and therefore have the same understanding they did. This guides us in correct interpretation.

Step two: Excavate the site

Once we have surveyed the general details of our site, that is, of the book of the Bible we are studying, we proceed with a series of excavations of the land. This will mean hard work with the pick and shovel and sometimes delicate work with a brush or cloth. We will divide the book into units of thought generally composed of a few verses and in some cases, a few paragraphs that make up a single *Field Study*. We will dig into the details of the biblical text in order to unearth its treasures.

We will use specific tools to discover the truth and significance of each passage. In most cases, the following elements will be the tools of our trade:

- **An outlined spacing analysis chart of the text.** This tool will help us ask and answer the question, *how is the text arranged?* We will focus on how the author structured the biblical text under the inspiration of the Holy Spirit. The arrangement of the unit we are studying is fundamental to discover the author's thought and purpose. It will help us to discern patterns, contrasts, emphases, progressions, conflicts, and arguments.

- **An explanation of what the passage says.** Here we will ask several different questions pertaining to our particular text. We will begin by asking, *what are the key terms?* We will examine key terms and phrases, identifying those elements in the passage which contribute most significantly to its meaning and message. We will then consider the question, *what is the explanation?*

Discoveries

Each *Field Study* ends with several pages of *Discoveries*. These are questions and exercises to help you remember and apply what you have learned from the biblical text. *Discoveries* have been designed to meet all learning styles. We learn by seeing, by hearing, and by doing. There are questions to discuss, exercises to write down, correlation between various biblical texts to make, and activities to do. They are provided to create the most effective learning experience for you.

Within this section, we may ask a question like, *what about the culture?* where we will consider cultural issues that enlighten us on the original audience of the text. If necessary we will ask, *what about the geography?* or *what about the history?* The Christian faith is a historical faith and therefore bound to time and space. Images, ideas, and cultural practices are all bound to a geo-location which reveal to us the richness of the treasure that lies beneath the dirt.

- **A historical contextual summary of the significance of the text.** After using all of these tools, we are finally ready to take the treasures we discovered and summarize them. In this section, we answer the question, *what is God saying?* Our response will present a brief summary of our findings and conclusions. Many times, this section will also provide us with other biblical examples that further help our understanding and reinforce the lessons we have learned.

- **A summary of the practical implications of the discoveries of our excavation.** We finish every excavation answering the question, *what does God want?* The purpose of these *Field Notes* is to encourage explorers to grow in their faith and live by it. Such faith is not alive unless the treasures we excavate become realities in our daily lives. We will provide for you some of the major principles discovered, along with particular suggestions for practical application. These suggestions are aids which will help you explore additional implications that may apply more significantly to your particular life story.

Step three: Analyze the find

Once you have completed digging through the biblical text, it is time to put down your tools and analyze what you have found. The Bible is God's revelation to humanity and is one grand story of his love for us. It is important that we analyze each book of the Bible in light of the rest of Scripture. Here is what you need to consider:

- **The place of this book within the biblical story.** Here we answer the question, *what does this book of the Bible contribute to the entire story of Scripture?* God wants us to learn about his nature and his character, and his plan for the ages, and each book of the Bible contributes to this understanding. This is why all of God's Word is valuable. It reveals the gracious nature of him who pursues us.

SAMPLE PAGES

This is the sidebar containing optional information to compliment and explain content from the main section.

This is the title bar showing the title, key theme, and the *Field Study* number.

The biblical text is always shown on an ancient scroll.

Timeline showing key events.

Note the use of pictures, maps, illustrations, and tables.

This is the main section of the page and contains all of the essential information.

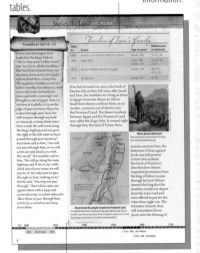

Footnotes are always used for biblical references.

- **The culmination of the story.** Finally, we answer the question, *how does the story end?* This helps us to understand each book of the Bible in light of the grand narrative.

- **The relationship of this book to Christ.** God's Word centers on the Lord Jesus Christ. His work of redemption opens up access to eternal life with God for those who believe. This is the gospel, the good news of Scripture. Our focus here is, *how does this book point to Christ?*

Understanding the design

Our *Field Notes* have been purposefully designed to enable you the explorer, to learn and apply more effectively the lessons of each passage you excavate. We strongly encourage you to invest some time in understanding the functionality of the design. This will greatly help your study and will make it more rewarding and enjoyable.

When using these *Field Notes*, please keep in mind the following principles:

- The notes are designed to provide as much relevant information as possible in an efficient way. You may not be able to study everything in one sitting, but you can know there is a wealth of information available for you in a single place. Come back to the study as often as you like and learn something new.

- Feel free to focus your attention in any of the different sections of the page and/or the sections of *Field Notes* as a whole. Everyone learns differently. Learn and apply that which best suits your learning style and your particular needs and interests, but challenge yourself to try something new.

- The main column of each page provides you with the essential content of the lesson. If you have limited time, we encourage you to focus your attention there. The items in the side margins are complementary to the main text and can be skipped if the material is already known.

- Blank spaces are provided in the margins. Use them to record your thoughts, observations, and questions. Make your own notes from the field.

The art of active learning

There are several things that you can do to help yourself learn new material. This is especially true with the Bible, so we have outlined five basic steps to help you engage in the learning process.

1. **Come prepared.** Begin by asking God for wisdom, humility, and dependence on the Holy Spirit to guide you into all truth. Pray, "*Open my eyes that I might see the wonderful things in your law*" from Psalm 119:18. Read with a pen or pencil in hand for marking the text or taking notes. Read aloud at times. This will help you engage your eyes, ears, and voice in the reading process.

2. **Preview the text.** Regardless of what you are going to read, quickly previewing the text will prepare your mind for what you are going to encounter. Look for a basic outline of the thought, the structure, and the key terms and concepts.

3. **Mark the text.** Use intentional, deliberate markings that fit your learning style. This will help you engage your mind in what you are reading and activate your memory. Here are some suggestions:
   - **Identify lists of related ideas or topics.** Itemize the list in the margin. Galatians 5:16–17 is a good example of a listing text.
   - **Mark key words and phrases.** The questions you ask from the text will guide you to key words or phrases. Repetition and contrast also point out key elements of the text.
   - **Identify relationships.** Mark logical relationships like *therefore*, *so that*, or *in order to*. Mark temporal relationships such as *before*, *after*, *the next day*, or *immediately*. Notate contrasts like *but* or *however*, and correlations like *if-then* or *either-or*. Also highlight conjunctions such as *and* or *or* as well as purpose statements like *for this reason*.

4. **Make notes.** Constantly summarize your ideas, write questions, repeat key words, use colors and symbols, and note references. Use your pen or pencil as a pointer so you will not lose your place. Find as many answers as possible to the six basic questions that unlock the content and meaning of a text: who, what, when, where, why, and how. Describe your thoughts completely, but be brief.

5. **Summarize, paraphrase, or outline the text.** Write a paragraph, sentence, or phrase to summarize what you have read in your own words. Reread the passage, paying attention to your markings and notes in the text so you will remember what you have read.

Colors and Symbols

Use a consistent color and/or symbol code that works for you.

- **Color parts of speech**—Use colors for nouns, pronouns, verbs and prepositions.
- **Color themes**—Use colors for key themes like God, faith, love or sin.
- **Color relationships**—Use colors for temporal or logical words like before, therefore, so that, or if-then.
- **Use Symbols**—Mark important concepts or characters with icons:
  - △ God – triangle
  - ♡ Love – heart
  - † Jesus – cross
  - ↶ Repentance – U-turn
  - ▯ Law – tablets
- **Use arrows**—indicate logical or temporal relationships.

Mix colors and symbols as needed but keep it simple and consistent.

Asking Questions

Who—is talking, is being spoken to, is acting, is obeying, is disobeying, is thinking, and is feeling?

What—is happening, is the lesson, must you avoid or imitate, is being said, is not said, did the person do, does the subject feel or think?

When—did this happen, will this happen?

Where—did it happen, is it happening, will it happen?

Why—did things happen, was something said or not said, was an action taken or avoided?

How—did things happen, will they happen, is the teaching illustrated, are conflicts caused or resolved?

Old Testament Scrolls

LAW

Genesis · Exodus · Leviticus · Numbers · Deuteronomy

HISTORY

Joshua · Judges · Ruth · First Samuel · Second Samuel · First Kings · Second Kings · First Chronicles · Second Chronicles · Ezra · Nehemiah · Esther

POETRY

Job · Psalms · Proverbs · Ecclesiastes · Song of Solomon

MAJOR PROPHETS

Isaiah · Jeremiah · Lamentations · Ezekiel · Daniel

MINOR PROPHETS

Hosea · Joel · Amos · Obadiah · Jonah · Micah · Nahum · Habakkuk · Zephaniah · Haggai · Zechariah · Malachi

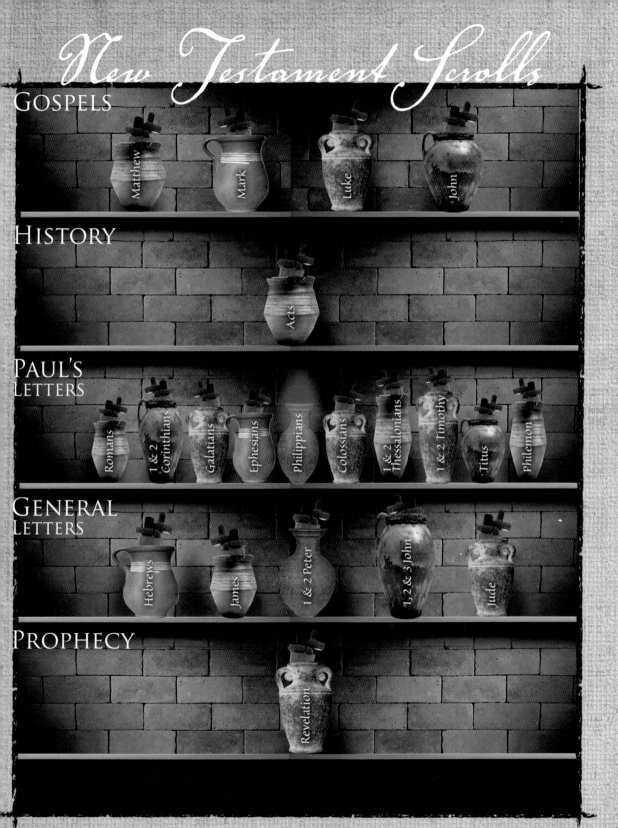

New Testament Scrolls

GOSPELS

Matthew · Mark · Luke · John

HISTORY

Acts

PAUL'S LETTERS

Romans · 1 & 2 Corinthians · Galatians · Ephesians · Philippians · Colossians · 1 & 2 Thessalonians · 1 & 2 Timothy · Titus · Philemon

GENERAL LETTERS

Hebrews · James · 1 & 2 Peter · 1, 2 & 3 John · Jude

PROPHECY

Revelation

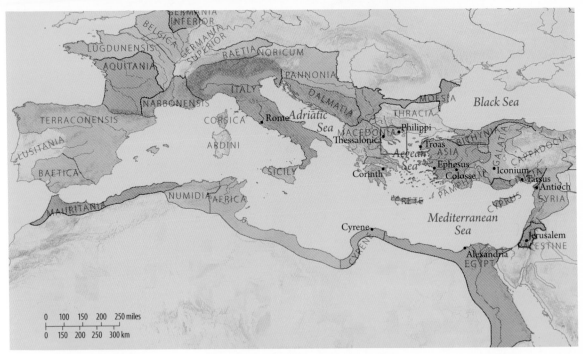

The Roman Empire

The Roman Empire provides the backdrop to much of the New Testament including Paul's missionary journeys recorded in the book of Acts. It was on Paul's second missionary journey that he first visited the city of Philippi and planted a church there.

The Setting of Philippians

Paul's letter to the Philippians was addressed to the first church he planted in present day Europe. He arrived in Philippi during his second missionary journey recorded in Acts 15:40–18:22. Paul was writing from prison, most likely in Rome.

Survey the Land
Philippians

Displaying God in godless times brings tension

Introduction
FIELD STUDY 1

Why should we study Philippians?

Like walking against a raging wind, living for God on Satan's turf is a treacherous endeavor. While Christians have the privilege of representing God on earth, they live in secular societies, which seek to conform them. Western cultures have become proud of *evolving* past *God* and no longer needing him. The pressure to accept the self-seeking values of a secular society and turn away from God are powerful and enticing everywhere we turn. We are fearful of being different and standing alone. We are lured into a self-fulfilling life of comfort, promotion, and pleasure without restraint or accountability. The ongoing secular sermon rings in our ears, preached aggressively across the media, the music industry, and social platforms. It's a message that says, "Truth and morality don't really matter after all, so live anyway you like. Just do it!" The pressures to embrace the worldview, values, practices, ambitions, hopes, and dreams of society and assimilate into a godless culture are many, varied, and sensually tempting. Life is much easier when giving in to fierce wind rather than trying to stand against it. Counter-cultural living is hard and deliberate. Living for God in Satan's domain inevitably brings tension.

Christians who cease to stand out begin to blend into their surrounding culture. When the mindset and values of secular society concerning lifestyles, faith, morality, responsibility, conduct, marriage, sexuality, and truth influence one's mind and take hold of one's heart they inevitably affect one's attitude and behavior. Society begins to influence the life and mission of the church rather than the

The World as Satan's Turf

Satan was defeated by the death and resurrection of Jesus Christ but still awaits destruction according to Revelation 20:10. Until then, God permits him to operate with a restricted rule over the world. For this reason, Satan is referred to as the *god of this world* in 2 Corinthians 4:4, and the *ruler of the kingdom of the air* in Ephesians 2:2.

The Christian Martyrs' Last Prayer
Christians have always faced fierce opposition from the culture around them. Many in the early church suffered despicable martyrdom, often in front of thousands, merely for the entertainment of the Roman elites.

Jean-Léon Gérôme, Acquired by William T. Walters, 1883

1

The Wonders of Christ

The wonder of a relationship with Christ is a reference to future hope experienced partly in the present. The believer in Christ is given purpose for life, support, and comfort through life, love in ways the world cannot fathom, and hope. Ultimately, that future hope is fulfilled in eternity in the presence of our Savior.

other way around. Not only does the fellowship of believers begin to look the same as the society in which they live, but the impact they are to make for Christ dissipates. Tragically, light gives way to darkness.

The book of Philippians addressed this same dilemma nearly two thousand years ago. Philippians is not a futuristic prophecy. It is simply a letter that shows awareness of the realities of life. Christians of every age have felt the pressure to compromise and conform to the patterns of this world. Yet God still wants his people to represent or display him, to live out what he values on earth and, by doing so, show the world the wonders of walking in close fellowship with him. Rather than taking the easy option of assimilating and conforming to society, God wants Christians to redeem and transform the world around them no matter the cost. Herein lies the importance of the book of Philippians. *This letter instructs us on how to live for God, modeling godly living under his rule as a heavenly colony in the midst of a godless culture.*

What is the background to our story?

The challenge of living for God in a godless world is not new. The history of mankind as recorded in the Scriptures testifies repeatedly to this. We will briefly survey the land of the biblical account, lining up some of the historical events, which lead to the writing of Philippians.

In Genesis, our first parents Adam and Eve, chose to do the very opposite of what God commanded. Though they knew God and walked with him, they rebelled against him rather than serving as his representatives on earth. Temptation knocked and they opened the door, only to experience the pain of life alienated from God. This story recurs through the first eleven chapters of Genesis. Those created with the privilege of representing God on earth flagrantly lived to oppose him. In these pages, we observe humanity as a whole, united in mindset and will against the merciful rule of God.[1]

God graciously committed himself to undo the work of sin by choosing a family through whom all the peoples of the earth would be

Tower of Babel

Genesis 11 is the account of a united mankind rebelling against God's command to scatter and fill the earth. The people built a tower that was to "reach the heavens" so that they could make a name for themselves. God crushed their rebellion by confusing their languages. They ended up being scattered over the entire earth.

Pieter Bruegel the Elder, 1563

1. Genesis 1:26; 3:6; 6:1–2, 5–6; 11:1–4

2091 God calls Abraham?

1925 God calls Abraham?

Receiving the Law on Mount Sinai? 1446

Receiving the Law on Mount Sinai? 1260

blessed. However, the members of this chosen family also failed him repeatedly. The patriarchs Abraham, Isaac, and Jacob walked with God but all too often gave into the pressures of society when things got tough. They feared man, lied, schemed, and cheated.[2]

The history of Israel, from the exodus out of Egypt to the return from Babylonian exile, demonstrates the tragedy of the yielding of God's people to the mindset and values of the pagan societies around them, rather than representing their God. Their failure is recorded from Exodus to Malachi in the Old Testament. God called Israel to represent him among the nations of the earth. He granted Israel the Law that communicated his values and desires for life.[3] As Israel walked with God obeying his law, the nations of the world would be enlightened and drawn to follow Abraham's God. Yet Israel continually chose to disobey. They worshipped false gods, embraced the immoral practices of the Canaanite societies, and conformed to the pattern of a godless world. In doing so, Israel became self-destructive and useless to God.

> ## Joshua 23:7–8
> Do not mix with these nations that remain among you. Do not invoke or swear by the names of their gods. Do not serve or bow down to them. But you are to hold tight to the LORD your God, as you have done until now.

> ## Exodus 19:5–6
> Now then, if you will indeed obey my voice and keep my covenant, then you will be my treasured possession out of all the nations, for the whole earth is mine, and you will be to me a kingdom of priests and a holy nation.

> ## Judges 2:19
> But when a judge died, they would turn back and become more corrupt than their fathers in following other gods to serve and bow down to them; they did not abandon their evil practices and stubborn ways.

Consider the stages of Israel's history. The first generation of Israelites desired the comforts of Egypt rather than follow God's leading to the Promised Land.[4] The generation that followed did a little better but still failed to obey God fully.[5] After that, the period of the Judges spiraled out of control as generation after generation of God's people were absorbed into the cultures around them and *did evil in the eyes of the Lord.*[6] The period of the monarchy began with God's representative nation desiring a king like the pagan nations around them.[7] King after king failed to lead God's people in a godly manner despite the urgent and persistent call of the prophets. Therefore, Israel received the reprimand that she was due. Through exile, God's people were

The Exile to Babylon
Watching their beloved Jerusalem burn while being hauled off into Babylonian exile was the ultimate humiliation for God's people. They thought that God would defend them regardless of their sin against him. Their actions reflected the pagan nations around them.

2. Genesis 12:10–20; 16:1–6; 25:29–34; 26:7; 27:18–19; 30:25–31:55
3. Exodus 20:1–20
4. Numbers 11:5
5. Joshua 15:63; 16:10; 17:13
6. Judges 3:7, 12; 4:16:1; 13:1
7. 1 Samuel 8:5

James Tissot, 1896–1902

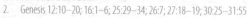

1250	1100	950	800	650	500 B.C.

Saul becomes king 1050

David becomes king 1010

Solomon becomes king 971

930 The kingdom divides

722 Northern kingdom falls to Assyria

Southern kingdom falls to Babylon and the temple is destroyed 586

3

absorbed into the nations of the earth.[1] When a remnant returned, it was not long before they conformed to the world again. The lesson of idolatry had not been fully learned.[2]

The New Testament record that precedes Philippians also bears testimony to the pressure experienced by followers of Jesus. His own disciples were easily attracted to the self-seeking values of the world.[3] Likewise, believers in Rome and Corinth had already been instructed concerning their conformity to worldly standards.[4]

The pressure of living for God within a pagan world is not new. This fact makes the divine message of Philippians particularly imperative for us today. We also face the same challenge between representing God on earth and being absorbed into society's way of life. We are just a little further along in human history. Let's explore what God says in this great book.

Who wrote this book?

The apostle Paul wrote the letter of Philippians and played a major role in the early church. He was God's chosen servant to spread the gospel to Gentile lands in accordance with the commission of Jesus in Acts 1:8. Paul was also God's instrument to write the explanation of the fulfillment of God's promised plan through Jesus Christ. Paul's writings in the New Testament are crucial to our understanding of how God's plan in history, expressed in the Old Testament, centers around Jesus.

Acts 1:8

But you will receive power when the Holy Spirit has come upon you, and you shall be my witnesses in Jerusalem, and in all Judea and Samaria, and to the end of the earth.

The Apostle Paul

Paul wrote the letter to the church at Philippi from prison. It seems most likely that it was written around A.D. 62 while the apostle was under house arrest in Rome as recorded in Acts 28:16, 30–31.

Rembrandt Harmenszoon van Rijn, 1633

Paul was a Jew born as *Saul* in the city of Tarsus and had the rare privilege of being both a Jew and a Roman citizen. Paul was skilled in tent-making and trained as a biblical scholar in Jerusalem under a famous Jewish intellectual named Gamaliel. He was also a zealous follower and guardian of the traditions of Judaism. However, God called him to serve Jesus Christ while on route to destroy Christianity in Damascus.[5] Through divine intervention, the most infamous persecutor of the Christian church became its most passionate preacher. By the time Philippians was written in the first century, Paul also

Shakko, 2007

The Emperor Nero

Nero Claudius Caesar Augustus Germanicus was the Roman Emperor from A.D. 54 to 68.

1. 2 Kings 17:7–41; 25
2. Ezra 10:1–44; Nehemiah 13:1–31
3. Mark 10:35–45
4. Romans 12:2; 1 Corinthians 3:1
5. Acts 9:1–22

B.C.	1	A.D.	10	20	30	40	50

5? Birth of Jesus

4–6? Birth of Paul

John the Baptist begins his ministry 28–29?

Jesus begins his ministry 28–30?

Jesus is crucified and resurrected 30–33?

33–34? Paul encounters Christ on Damascus road

46–47? First Missiona Journey by Pa

became Christianity's most prolific scholar and spokesperson.

What was going on at the time?

When Paul wrote the letter to the Philippians, he was under house arrest in Rome. Paul was awaiting a hearing before the ruler of

The Mamertine Prison
According to tradition, the Mamertime Prison in Rome is where Paul was incarcerated. This probably was the case later on in Paul's life but not during Paul's first confinement in Rome when he wrote Philippians. According to Acts 28:30, Paul was in a rented house, and most likely endured two separate imprisonments in Rome in the A.D. 60's.

the Roman Empire—a Caesar named Nero. The Roman state was struggling to understand and deal with Christianity. Judaism was a legal religion under Rome, or a *religio licita*, and Christianity seemed to be a type of Judaism to the Roman authorities.[6] The confusing issue for the Romans was that Judaism adamantly opposed Christianity. Why were Jews so outraged at the Christian teachings of a Jewish scholar called Paul? Perhaps more importantly, was it true that Christians worshipped a human-god other than the Roman Caesar? That was treason!

As Paul was undergoing the hardship of imprisonment in Rome, he received a financial gift from believers in the Roman city of Philippi who were also undergoing difficulties. The Philippians lived in a Roman culture, saturated with Roman values and religious beliefs. Paul wrote this letter, to thank the Philippians for their gift, but also to provide these Christians with much needed encouragement and direction regarding their Christian living in an anti-Christian environment. These Christians were struggling to live boldly for the

Lord Jesus Christ in a society ruled by *lord Caesar*—the same ruler Paul was waiting to boldly preach Christ to in Rome.

The Philippian believers felt the pressure of a society that flagrantly rejected Jesus Christ. Blending in or being a secret Christian was a more enticing option than being socially ridiculed, marginalized, imprisoned or even killed. However, their problems were also self-inflicted by their adoption of the customs of the culture. Some Philippians lived without restraint and came to embrace the

***Via Egnatia* through Philippi**
The Egnatian Way or *Via Egnatia* was the main Roman road running east-west across the empire. You can still see the remains of the road amongst the ruins of Philippi.

6. Acts 25:19, 27

49? Jerusalem Council

50–52? Second Missionary Journey by Paul

60–62? Paul arrives in Rome under house arrest

64 Fire in Rome

70 Temple is destroyed

79 Pompeii and Herculaneum are destroyed by Vesuvius eruption

John writes Revelation 95–96?

Controlling Philippi

Military leaders, kings, and would-be kings long recognized the value of controlling Philippi.

- King Philip II of Macedon, father of Alexander the Great, conquered Krenides, renaming it Philippi, in 356 B.C. Its location formed a natural defense against invasions into Greece.
- Roman generals Octavian and Mark Antony defeated the assassins of Julius Caesar and generals Brutus and Cassius, in the Battle of Philippi in 42 B.C. They allowed Roman soldiers to retire and colonize Philippi.
- After Octavian defeated Mark Antony he sent more Roman soldiers to colonize Philippi. In 30 B.C., Octavian wanted to dilute any potential allegiance the veterans of the Battle of Philippi may have had to Mark Antony.
- Octavian became Caesar Augustus, the founder of the Roman Empire and first emperor until his death in A.D. 14.

values, ambitions, wants, and desires of their godless society. These Philippians were true Christians, but they were also becoming self-centered among one another despite their generous giving to ministry. Selfishness and self-promotion were acceptable attitudes in a culture whose ruler had an inflated sense of self, but not in the eyes of God. Self-centered living was causing disunity among God's people in Philippi and that was not befitting of God's representatives.

Who was the audience?

The letter of Philippians was written to Christians in the Roman city of Philippi in the Roman province of Macedonia. The geographical location of Philippi had long been recognized as of strategic military and economic importance. It was situated close to gold mines and guarded an important ancient roadway, which the Romans had built into their famous Egnatian Way. The mountains to the north and sea to the south funneled travelers, traders, and armies through the plains just below Philippi.

By the middle of the first century, Philippi was fully recognized as a Roman city. This means that it had the rare privilege of being a Roman colony city—a sort of Rome away from Rome. Thus, it was treated as if it was located on Italian soil. In fact, it had been colonized over the last century by retired Roman army soldiers and had a Roman garrison watching over it. There were no doubts in Philippi as to whom their allegiance belonged.

Acts 16:6–40 records God's concern for the people of Philippi. Therefore, he directed Paul to the province of Macedonia during his second missionary journey so that this region would hear the gospel.[1] After a few days in Philippi, Paul and his companions Timothy, Silas, and probably Luke, proclaimed the good news of Christ by the river to a God-fearing lady named Lydia. She became a Christian along

1. Acts 15:41–18:22

42	Battle of Philippi
30	Soldiers colonize Philippi
27	Caesar Augustus begins rule

Birth of Paul 4–6?

with her household.[2] Sometime later, the city's jailer together with his household also became Christians. This was the beginning of the Philippian church. The apostle wrote the letter of Philippians to address the beloved church he had founded some ten years earlier.

When did this happen?

The evidence suggests that Philippians was likely written around A.D. 62 while Paul was imprisoned.[3] The most prolonged and best known of his many imprisonments were in Caesarea Maritima and Rome.[4] However, in this letter, Paul mentions both Caesar's elite troops hearing the gospel and the Emperor's personal staff sending greetings.[5] He also speaks as if he has reached the last phase of the legal process that Roman citizens like him were entitled to; a hearing before Caesar in Rome, which could result in his death.[6] Therefore, Rome is the most probable location from which Paul writes this letter. He was held captive there for two years from A.D. 60–62.[7] Since Paul speaks confidently that he will be released soon, it is likely Philippians was written at the end of this two-year period.[8]

Roman Theater

Philippi contained all of the typical features of a Roman city including a Roman Theatre. One of the support pillars of this theatre contains the *"Victoria Augusta"* which commemorates the victory of Octavian and Mark Antony over the assassins of Julius Caesar in 42 B.C.

Todd Bolen, www.BiblePlaces.com

How should we read this type of book?

There are three important issues to understand before we start digging into the meaning of Philippians. Paul mentions these in the letter without explanation since they were part of everyday Roman life. The Philippian believers would have noticed what Paul was expressing, but we on the other hand, live in a different time and age, so we need a little help. Consider the following as a lens through which to see with more clarity the message and significance of the letter. Remember them as you excavate the text in the upcoming *Field Studies*.

Prison Epistles

The word *epistle* is the Greek word for *letter*. The New Testament books of Ephesians, Philippians, Colossians, and Philemon are often referred to as the Prison Epistles. This is because they are traditionally considered to have been written while Paul was under the same imprisonment in Rome.

2. Acts 16:13–15
3. Philippians 1:7, 13, 17
4. 2 Corinthians 6:5; 11:23; Acts 24:27;
5. Philippians 1:13; 4:22
6. Philippians 1:19–26; 2:17
7. Acts 28:11–31
8. Philippians 2:24

Roman Citizenship

This is a drawing of a bronze plaque recording the grant of Roman citizenship to men from Hispania in reward for their service as Roman cavalry.

J.M de la rosa, 1908

20	30	40	50	60	70	A.D.

Jesus is crucified and resurrected 30–33?

Paul's First Missionary Journey 46–47?

Paul's first Roman imprisonment 60–62?

Paul encounters Christ on Damascus road 33–34?

Paul's Caesarea imprisonment 58–60?

Paul's second Roman imprisonment and death 67?

Paul's Second Missionary Journey 50–52?

Roman Citizenship

Roman citizenship was granted on several grounds. The obvious and most respected reason was birth to parents who were citizens. Liberated slaves of citizens, soldiers discharged from the auxiliary Roman army after 25 years of service, the payment of huge sums of money, and actions deemed of special service to the Empire could all lead to citizenship. Given Paul's parents were Jews, it is likely they received citizenship as a reward for special service. In any case, all inhabitants of Tarsus, Paul's hometown, received citizenship in 66 B.C. This is why Paul could say he was born a citizen granting him a very respected type of Roman citizenship in Acts 22:28.

Philo of Alexandria

The first century A.D. Jewish writer Philo refers to Moses as, *"a model for all those who were inclined to imitate him . . . for indeed, there is no one who does not know that men in a lowly condition are imitators of men of high reputation, and that what they see, these last chiefly desire, towards that do they also direct their own inclinations and endeavors."*
(Philo De Vita Mosis 1.158–160)

André Thevet, 1584

The first concept to understand is the importance of *Roman citizenship*. Philippi was a Roman colony and the members of the church there knew the high value of possessing Roman citizenship. Citizenship signaled status and status was highly valued by all. It could be said that each inhabitant of Philippi was one of two kinds: a citizen or one who wished to be a citizen. However, citizenship in the first century was still an honor bestowed on few. It brought status because it granted standing with privilege and responsibility. A citizen enjoyed tax reliefs, access to recreational events, security, and legal protection. The greatest privilege, which everyone was eager for, was high standing in the social hierarchy. If you were a citizen, you were known in town and noticed on the street.

One of the advantages of granting citizenship was that it created unity and loyalty to Rome across large land areas and diverse people groups. Therefore, Rome was represented and promoted across the Empire by these privileged few. Representing Rome well was the responsibility of Roman citizens. Citizens were to live worthy of their status because the greatness of Rome was on display through them. Paul employs this coveted status in his letter to the Philippians to encourage them to live in light of a much more valuable status: their heavenly citizenship. He wanted Christians to understand that heavenly citizens have many privileges and responsibilities too. They get to display the greatness of their God and his values on earth. So read Philippians with these questions in mind: Whom do I represent? In what or in whom does my sense of value and identity lie? What are the values I get to display?

The second essential issue to understand in studying Philippians concerns *role models*. In the letter, Paul uses a well-known teaching model of imitation to instruct the Philippian Christians. Both the Romans and the Jews used this way of educating others known as *imitatio*. Students or disciples copied the skills, practices, character, and lifestyle of the person they wanted to imitate. After all, the instructor was the embodiment of what he knew and believed. *Showing* others how to live life in the desired way was more effective than *telling* them how to do it.

Seneca the Younger, a tutor to the Roman Emperor Nero, made the following statement:
> "The living voice and the intimacy of a common life will help you more than the written word. You must go to the scene of the action, first, because men put more faith in their eyes than in their ears, and second, because the way is long if one follows precepts, but short and helpful, if one follows patterns... It was not the classroom of Epicurus, but living together under the same

roof, that made great men of Metrodorus, Hermarchus, and Polyaenus."

(Seneca Epistles: On Sharing Knowledge 6.5–7 translated by Richard M. Gummere)

Paul's exhortation to Christians to live worthy of their heavenly citizenship is constructed according to the helpful teaching model of *imitatio*. Paul shows Christians how to live a worthy Christian life by presenting Christ, Timothy, Epaphroditus, and himself as role models to *imitate*. In doing so, the letter of Philippians constitutes an invitation for us to consider whom we should aspire to be like.

Lucius Annaeus Seneca

This statue of Seneca is a sculpture by Puerta de Almodóvar in Córdoba, Spain. Often known as Seneca the Younger, he lived from around 4 BC – AD 65 as a Roman philosopher and statesman.

The final issue to understand in Philippians is the *worship of the emperor as a human-god*. The Romans understood that masses of people from many backgrounds could be controlled through religion. Therefore, the Roman Caesar was considered *Lord and Savior* in colonial cities such as Philippi. The Philippians enjoyed leisure at theaters and sporting events, security and justice in the law courts and police stations, basic sanitation in public baths and toilets, as well as access to the gods at temples. This was all because their allegiance was to Rome through submission to Caesar as Lord and Savior. People could have other gods, but Caesar was also to be confessed and worshipped as a son of the gods.

This made life hard for Christians. How could they live daily in a city where their exclusive allegiance to Jesus was put to the test at every turn? What would living counter-culturally involve? What would happen to Christians when the Roman Empire would understand that Christianity worshipped another Son of God as Lord and Savior? This was the God-man

Imitation

In the first century A.D. the historian Dionysius of Halicarnassus wrote a three part work called *De Imitatio*. Only fragments of this work have survived, some of which were quoted within the writings of the ancient writer Syrianus. Fortunately, one of the surviving fragments states: *"Imitation leads to the likeness of the individual desired…"*

(De Imitatio fragment 6.1)

Pantheon in Rome

The Pantheon in Rome was originally built by Marcus Agrippa in 31 B.C. and later rebuilt by Emperor Hadrian around A.D. 126. As a temple to all the gods of ancient Rome, it represented the challenge for believers to exclusively worship Christ.

Giovanni Paolo Panini, 1692–1765

20   30   40   50   60   70 A.D.

Jesus is crucified and resurrected 30–33?

Paul encounters Christ on Damascus road 33–34?

Paul's First Missionary Journey 46–47?

Paul's Second Missionary Journey 50–52?

Paul's Caesarea imprisonment 58–60?

Paul's first Roman imprisonment 60–62?

Paul's second Roman imprisonment and death 67?

9

Ancient Letters

There were many types of letters in the world of the first century A.D. Philippians blends what would be considered a friendship letter with a family letter. The Philippian believers are friends of Paul but their common bond in Christ makes them brothers and sisters too. Ancient letters followed an established format. These are some of the major features they included:

1. Introduction:
   It names the writer and the recipient and it contains a greeting and either a word of thanksgiving, or a prayer of thanksgiving.
2. Main body:
   It deals with the issue that caused the letter to be written.
3. Conclusion:
   It expresses final greetings, perhaps a description of how the letter was written—with the assistance of a scribe or not—and a benediction.

Outline of Philippians

Opening 1:1–2
Thanksgiving and Prayer 1:3–11
Paul's Situation 1:12–26
Appeal with Examples 1:27–4:1
   Central Appeal 1:27–2:4
   Example 1: Jesus 2:5–11
   Example 2 and 3:
      Timothy & Epaphroditus
      2:12–30
   Example 4: Paul 3:1–4:1
Philippian Situation 4:2–9
Thanksgiving 4:10–20
Closing 4:21–23

called Jesus who was a Jew executed by the Romans on a cross. At the time of the writing of Philippians, this tension had not yet spilled over into full-blown physical persecution, but the situation for Christians in all spheres of daily life had already become tense. In Philippians, Paul encourages Christians to be willing to worship Jesus alone in a society with tempting and convenient alternatives.

Why did God give us this message?

Why does God want you to explore this letter? What relevance does it have for your life today? The tensions and temptations the Philippian Christians faced many years ago remain. The way in which God wants believers to live in the midst of such difficulty also remains.

With this in mind, here are a few applicational questions for you to think through before going deeper in this study. Prepare for digging into the text by digging a little into your own heart first. Take time to consider them both from a personal and church viewpoint.

How does society influence you?

People act according to what they value. *We are value-driven people.* Moreover, values are always shaped and influenced by some kind of authority. If God is not shaping a society's values then who is? If someone other than God is shaping a society's mindset, how does that society in turn continually influence its individuals? Television, radio, music, the media, fashion, famous role models, secular universities, are not always inherently evil but we must be aware of how a society's values are shaped because we are members of society. So how is society influential? How are you influenced by it?

Do you find it difficult to live exclusively for Christ?

What are some of the spiritual tensions you face in life? What are some of the situations in which your commitment to God is put to the test? When and where do these usually occur? Why do you think that is the case? How much are you enticed by that which competes with Christ? Write down some of the pressures you think a Christian faces by living for Christ on Satan's turf. Take time to think carefully about these questions before you continue with your study.

Discoveries

Now that you have completed the *survey* into the rich soil of Philippians, it is time to consider what you have learned. Choose the questions that are most helpful to you or your group.

Connecting with the community

These group questions are designed to help you apply what God wants from you. When applicable, think of these questions not only as an individual but also in terms of your family, your community, your nation, and your church.

1. Why is it important to understand the biblical, historical, and theological background of Philippians before reading the text of this epistle?

2. After reading this introductory *Field Study,* what is the most important reason to study this New Testament letter?

3. These *Field Notes* on Philippians are subtitled, "*Displaying God in godless times.*" What does this mean specifically?

4. At the beginning of our study, we describe how difficult it is to live exclusively for God in the midst of a godless society. Why is this true? What aspects of the culture that you live in are most destructive to the zeal and devotion of Christians?

5. Consider you own life. What aspects of society do you find more enticing and tempting? What is it about the world that you have a tendency to admire and love?

6. Recall the various stories presented in the news during the past few months. Has Christianity been attacked or mocked in any way? If so, what was the cause behind such belligerence? How did the Christians involved react? Are their reactions *godly*?

7. Where was the apostle Paul when he wrote this letter? Why was he in that location? How was Paul's condition relevant to the message of the letter he wrote to the Philippians?

8. Review the section "*What is the background to our story?*" Of the different examples showing the tendency of the people of God to compromise and embrace worldly practices, which one do you find most enlightening and why?

9. Who were the Philippians? Describe some particular characteristics of the beliefs and practices of the culture in the city of Philippi. How are these relevant to the message of the letter?

10. On a scale of 1 to 10, with 1 representing a little and 10 representing a lot, rate your present knowledge of the book of Philippians. At the end of *Field Study 9*, you will have another opportunity to evaluate your knowledge in light of what you have learned.

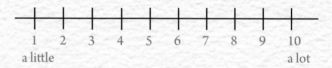

Probing deeper

These exercises are for your continued study of some of the key issues in Philippians. They will require you to look at other passages beyond the text of Philippians and should to be thought of in terms of yourself, your family, your community, your nation, and your church.

1. Explain the relationship between the books of Acts and Philippians. Why is it helpful to refer to Acts when beginning a study of Philippians?

2. Read the account of the beginning of the church in Philippi in Acts 16:11–40. Make two lists, one noting the theme of suffering and the other noting the theme of joy. These themes are not just part of the story of the founding of the Philippian church but also significant in this letter written to these same believers around ten years later.

3. Who was the apostle Paul? Skim through Acts 9 through 28 and list the apostle's circumstances during his missionary journeys and imprisonments. How does his personal experience with suffering and persecution make him an ideal person to address the issues that were causing trouble to the church of Philippi?

4. Compile a list of ways in which the culture influences you away from Christ. Discuss you list with someone who knows you well. Do you have blind spots where you are not seeing the influence of your society? How can you be more aware of what pulls you away from Christ?

Bringing the story to life

Learning biblical geography helps us to understand the context of the Bible. Locate each of the following features on the map and label them. See the map on page xiv at the beginning of your *Field Notes* for help.

- **Countries and Regions**: Asia, Bithynia, Cappadocia, Cilicia, Crete, Cyprus, Egypt, Galatia, Italy, Macedonia, Palestine, Pamphylia, Sicily, Syria, and Thracia.

- **Cities**: Alexandria, Antioch, Colosse, Corinth, Cyrene, Ephesus, Iconium, Jerusalem, Philippi, Rome, Tarsus, Thessalonica, and Troas.

- **Water**: Adriatic Sea, Aegean Sea, Black Sea, and the Mediterranean Sea.

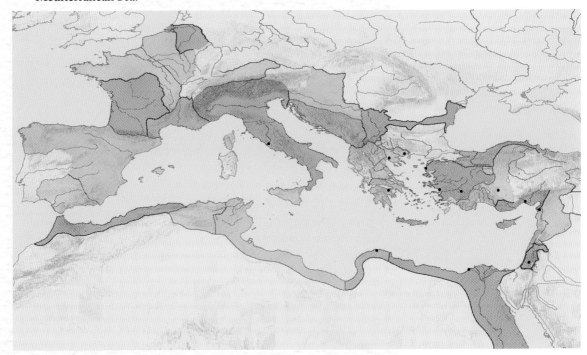

Memorizing the key
Commit to memory the key phrase for Philippians, which is:

> Displaying God in godless times brings tension

Part of learning the Bible is remembering what the Bible is about and where to find things. Memorizing the key phrases will help you to better understand and apply the key points of each book.

Observation journaling
This section will prepare you for *Field Study* 2. You will read through the first section of the book of Philippians. We have included three types of exercises: some for before you read, some for while you are reading and some for after you have completed the reading.

Before you read
Discuss and fill in the chart below with what you already know about Paul's letter to the Philippians. This exercise will help you learn and remember as you encounter new information. You will fill in the new information after you have read the text.

Reading knowledge chart

	What I already know	What I have learned
What is the problem in the Philippian church?		
What is Paul saying about the problem?		

While you are reading
On the following page, the biblical text is laid out with a wide margin so you can mark the text with questions, key terms, notes, and structures. The verse markings have been removed so you can read it without distractions and have laid out the text with some spacing to help you see how the lines are related. Review the guidelines on *The art of active learning* section, page xi at the beginning of your *Field Notes* for some suggestions on reading, learning, and marking the text effectively.

• Philippians 1:1–11

Paul and Timothy, slaves of Christ Jesus, to all the saints in Christ Jesus who are in Philippi, with the overseers and deacons: Grace and peace to you from God our Father and the Lord Jesus Christ.

I thank my God every time I remember you. I always pray with joy in all my prayers for all of you, because of your partnership in the gospel from the first day until now. For I am confident of this very thing, that he who began a good work in you will bring it to completion until the day of Christ Jesus. It is right for me to feel this way about all of you, because I have you in my heart, since both in my imprisonment and in the defense and confirmation of the gospel, you are all partners of God's grace with me. For God is my witness, how I long for you all with the affection of Christ Jesus.

And this I pray, that your love may abound more and more in knowledge and all discernment so that you can discern what is excellent, and thus be sincere and blameless for the day of Christ Jesus, filled with the fruit of righteousness that comes through Jesus Christ, to the glory and praise of God.

Notes, Observations & Questions

Summarize the text here

After you have read

1. Go back to your *reading knowledge chart* on page 14 and fill in anything that you have learned while reading through this first section of Philippians. Compare it with what you already knew to see what the text has revealed so far.

2. Journaling Scripture is another way to help us learn and is modeled in Deuteronomy 17:18. You will remember more if you respond to what you have read by writing. Therefore, write out Philippians 1:1–11 from the previous page or from your own Bible into a journal word for word. Once completed, journal your thoughts on godly living in a godless culture.

3. Now read Philippians 1:1–11 in your own Bible. Continue to reread it each day until you get to *Field Study 2*. This will reinforce the learning of Scripture and help you to better retain its message.

Pray

As we learn the word of God, it is essential that we communicate with him through prayer. Commit to praying throughout the week alone or with others, asking God to help you identify areas in your life where you are allowing society to negatively influence you. Write your own prayer or use this as a sample prayer:

Dear Heavenly Father,

I'm excited about studying your word in greater depth through the book of Philippians. I realize that I am vulnerable to the influences of a society that opposes you unless I am continually feasting on what you have said in your word. Only by knowing you through your word will I overcome the patterns of this world and be transformed into who you want me to be. Help me dig through this study listening to you as you have spoken through Paul. I desire to be influenced only by you so that I can live my life exclusively for you. Open my eyes to see the corruption of society and your beauty. Teach me to live as a Christian in the midst of this world ruled by Satan. Transform me so I can represent you well. Soften my heart to see my sins and confess them. Cover my sins with the blood of Jesus. I submit myself to you and what you want to teach me in this book. In the precious name of Christ I pray, Amen.

Excavate the Site
Philippians 1:1–11
Praise God, he is still at work!

Philippians 1:1–11
FIELD STUDY 2

How is the text arranged?

We now begin our exploration of the letter to the Philippians in order to discover its contribution to the overall message of the Bible. This study excavates the first eleven verses. Read the text several times in your own Bible. See if you can identify its structure before looking at the one provided:

Philippians 1:1–11

Section	Bible Text
Opening words (1:1–2)	
Author	¹Paul and Timothy, slaves of Christ Jesus,
Recipients	to all the saints in Christ Jesus who are in Philippi, with the overseers and deacons.
Greeting	²Grace and peace to you from God our Father and the Lord Jesus Christ.
Expression of Thanksgiving (1:3–8)	
Reason 1	³I thank my God every time I remember you. ⁴I always pray with joy in all my prayers for all of you ⁵because of your partnership in the gospel from the first day until now.
Reason 2	⁶For I am confident of this very thing, that he who began a good work in you will bring it to completion until the day of Christ Jesus.
Reason 3	⁷It is right for me to feel this way about all of you, because I have you in my heart, since both in my imprisonment and in the defense and confirmation of the gospel you are all partners of God's grace with me.

Arranging the Text

Visually arranging the text in this outline helps us to appreciate the progress in Paul's reasoning. The indentation of phrases and sentences helps to illustrate the relationships among them.

Philippians 1:1–11

Section	Bible Text
Reason 3 (continued)	[8] For God is my witness, how I long for you all with the affection of Christ Jesus.
Prayer (1:9–11)	
Petition of growth	[9] And this I pray, that your love may abound more and more in knowledge and all discernment [10] so that you can discern what is excellent, and thus be sincere and blameless for the day of Christ Jesus, [11] filled with the fruit of righteousness that comes through Jesus Christ to the glory and praise of God.

From the guide above, we observe that the first passage in Philippians is an introduction to the letter. Paul's opening words present the expected identification of author, recipients, and greeting. He then includes an expression of thanksgiving and gives the reasons for his gratitude to God for the Philippian believers. This leads finally to the content of the prayer Paul raises before God on behalf of these Christians.

What is this passage saying?
What are some key terms and phrases?
Now that you have a basic idea of its main flow, let's dig a little deeper into the content. Here are some key terms, phrases, issues, or concepts useful to understanding the meaning and significance of the passage.

Meaning of Key Terms

Key word or phrase	Meaning and significance
Pray with joy (1:4)	In Philippians, Paul mentions the word *joy*, or a derivative of it like *rejoice*, on 16 occasions. Clearly the apostle deems joy very important for the Philippians since this book contains about half of all the occurrences of the word in Paul's writings. Exhibiting the attitude of joy is obviously an important Christian trait. Joy is a fruit of the Spirit (Galatians 5:22; Romans 14:17). Joy is more than an emotion, though it is expressed sometimes as one.

A Reputation for Joy

Is your church known for it's joy? The church in Philippi was in the region of Macedonia. Paul mentions in 2 Corinthians 8:1–2 that the Macedonian churches were known for their joy in the midst of hardship. What a great reputation to have.

Meaning of Key Terms

Key word or phrase	Meaning and significance
Pray with joy (*continued*)	Joy can be described as a state, attitude, or condition a believer exhibits no matter the circumstances because his or her focus is not fixed on a situation but on God. Even though Christians experience suffering, grief, and hardship, they can do so with joy because of their belief that God is in control, that he cares for them, and that he will complete his work in history through Christ. Therefore, joy is a distinctive mark of a Christian who understands the bigger picture of God's eternal purpose. On the other hand, a joyless Christian is one whose focus has shifted from hope in Christ to personal circumstances. This can easily occur and lead to bitterness and a sense of disappointment and hopelessness. God's desire is that his people are characterized by joy. As you read this letter, note the circumstances in which Paul calls for joy.
Saints (1:1) but he who began a good work in you will bring it to completion (1:6)	The apostle Paul often calls believers *saints* (see 2 Corinthians 1:1; Ephesians 1:1; Colossians 1:1; Philemon 5, 7). At times, he declares that they are *called to be saints*, which means that they have a responsibility to live according to their true character in Christ (Romans 1:7; 1 Corinthians 1:2). The implication of this is that though believers *are* saints, they might not live accordingly. This was the situation, for example, in the Corinthian church. In Philippians 1:1–11, it is clear Paul believes saints are still in process. They are imperfect saints. How is this possible? What we have here is an expression of an important Christian truth, which all believers need to understand. When a person trusts in Jesus Christ for salvation, he or she is *declared* righteous by God; blameless on account of the righteousness of Jesus. That person is a saint *positionally* before God. As one lives the Christian life, God desires to *transform* that person by the power of the Spirit into someone who is becoming a saint in *practice*. The declared saint is being transformed into a saint. It is for this reason that Paul can call the Philippians saints on the one hand, and yet on the other hand acknowledge that they are not yet perfected. The Philippian believers then, like us today, are saints who are still being perfected.
The day of Christ Jesus (1:6, 10)	Paul anticipates a time in every believer's future when he or she will directly encounter Jesus Christ. Given the diverse descriptions of this day in the New Testament, there are differences of opinion concerning the meaning of *day* (see Acts 2:16–21; 1 Corinthians 1:8; 5:5; 2 Corinthians 1:14; 1 Thessalonians 3:12–13; 5:2; 2 Thessalonians 2:1–12). There are also questions about the role the Old Testament concept of the "day of the Lord" plays in its understanding (Joel 2:1–11; Amos 5:18–20). Furthermore, some are influenced by their interpretation regarding the order of the events of the end times—called *eschatology*.

1 – Saints Justified

The act of being declared righteous by God due to faith in Christ is referred to in the New Testament as *justification* (Romans 3:24; 5:1–2; 6:23; Galatians 2:16; Ephesians 2:8–9; 1 Peter 2:24). Justification grants eternal life and occurs the instant one believes in Jesus. He or she is now forever free from the penalty of sin.

2 – Saints Sanctified

Beginning with justification, the believer is in the process of being made righteous by the power of the Spirit. This process is called *sanctification*. The one declared holy or justified in status is being transformed day by day to become holy in practice by walking in the Spirit (Galatians 5:16–26). The saint liberated from the penalty of sin is learning to live free of the power of sin.

3 – Saints Glorified

Only when a believer comes before God in heaven will he or she actually become fully righteous, thus experiencing *glorification* (Romans 8:30; 1 Corinthians 15:42–44; 51–53). The one declared holy, and who was also being made holy is now completely holy, experiencing the culmination of salvation—a sinless life with God. Only then will the believer be completely free from the penalty, power, and presence of sin.

The Corinthian Example

The Corinthian Christians are an example of how believers have a calling to be saints yet fail to live accordingly. Paul wrote the letter of 1 Corinthians in order to exhort these believers to *practically* live out their *position* in Christ. According to 1 Corinthians 1:2, the Corinthians were sanctified saints in that they had been set apart by God as his children and to his service. However, they were living as though they were still under the power of sin (1 Corinthians 3:1–3; 5:1). God's will is to perfect those whom he has declared holy.

Meaning of Key Terms

Key word or phrase	Meaning and significance
The day of Christ Jesus *(continued)*	In this passage, Paul expresses his desire for the Philippian believers to grow in sanctification because of their future encounter with Christ. Later in his letter, Paul will express his desire that they grow so that *he* can be pleased before Christ on that day as well (2:16). Elsewhere, Paul refers to believers' future encounter with Christ as judge over their lives (2 Corinthians 5:10; Romans 14:10). For the believer, this meeting will expose which works merit God's reward (1 Corinthians 3:13–15). It is important to note, that this *day* is a reward ceremony for faithfulness and service to Christ. It will be a joyful event with room for perhaps a little bit of temporary *healthy* regret that we did not serve him more. Paul refers to this event as "the judgment seat of Christ" in 2 Corinthians 5:10. The image is borrowed from the common fixture of a judgment seat in public squares and sporting arenas of the time. It was simply a raised platform often with a seat used by an official addressing a crowd mainly when passing a judgment but also as part of reward ceremonies at the close of sporting events—perhaps like our modern day Olympics.

What about the culture?

There are two background issues to examine in comprehending this passage. The first is an understanding of ancient letters and the second relates to slavery, as the Philippians would have understood it.

Philippians is an ancient letter and must be read as one. Introductions to these letters contained standard elements like the name of the writer, the recipients, a personal greeting, and a health wish much like our structured ways of beginning formal and informal letters today. Paul generally followed these conventions even though at times he modified them to his own purposes.[1] For example, the first verses in Philippians note the senders, recipients, and contain a greeting. However, Paul wrote most of his letters for public reading. His letters to a church or churches were read aloud in the presence of the believers. Therefore, Paul also incorporates conventions expected in public speaking.

In Philippians, Paul adapts what would be considered a health wish and prayer. He makes them function as the initial part in a public

Christ before Pilate

Here Pilate sits in the judgment seat as Christ is brought before him on trial. While the context in this case is condemnation, the same judgment seat was also used for commendation for faithful service which is what the Apostle Paul has in mind in Philippians.

Mihály Munkácsy 1881

1. Ephesians 1:1–3; Colossians 1:1–8

B.C.	1	A.D.	10	20	30	40	50

5? Birth of Jesus

4–6? Birth of Paul

John the Baptist begins his ministry 28–29?

Jesus begins his ministry 28–30?

Jesus is crucified and resurrected 30–33?

33–34? Paul encounters Christ on Damascus road

46–47? First Missionary Journey by Pau

address where a speaker would establish a connection and credibility with his audience. This was called an *exordium* and included a preview of the main issues to be discussed. Paul clearly lays bare his emotions for the Philippian believers as if he was in their presence and reminds them of their close bond. Did you notice the passion in his words? Other issues to emerge are attitude and conduct, responsibility and diversity in Christian service, accountability to God, love for one another, and growth in maturity in Christ. Paul is preparing his readers for issues he will deal with later in the epistle.

(1) In the first verse of the letter, Paul calls himself a slave. Roman audiences like the Philippians would have been shocked by this self-degrading designation, particularly since Paul was a Roman citizen. The Roman world of the first century A.D. was a slave society. This meant that slavery was legal, rampant, morally unquestioned, essential to society, and economically useful. If slavery were abolished, the Roman way of life would collapse. Slaves were not just the backbone of the Roman economy but also of everyday life. They farmed the land, mined the quarries, and birthed, raised, and educated the children. Slaves were necessary, self-sacrificing servants. They were the doctors, cooks, bakers, barbers, and civil administrators. Despite their indispensability, slaves had little status in a Roman society where status was highly regarded.

Galatians 3:28
There is neither Jew nor Greek, there is neither slave nor free, there is neither male nor female, for you are all one in Christ Jesus.

Slaves were at the bottom of the prized social hierarchy, which everyone wanted to climb. They were deemed as *speaking instruments* or *instrumentum vocale*. War captives were the main source of slaves who were then bought and sold at the market as goods with warranties (often 6 months) and varying prices depending on gender, physical condition, nationality, and genetics. In labeling himself a slave, Paul does not just

Seneca on Slavery
In the first century A.D. Lucius Annaeus Seneca wrote about a proposal that was defeated in the Roman Senate to have slaves wear clothing that would distinguish them in public for they often physically looked no different than free persons. The proposal was rejected for fear that if slaves could so easily identify how many of them there were in Rome they may be tempted to join forces and rebel.
(Seneca De Clementia 1.24.1)

Peter Paul Rubens, 1605

Ancient Example of a Secular Letter

Polycrates to his father

GREETING.   *Greeting*

I AM GLAD IF YOU ARE IN   *Health wish*
GOOD HEALTH, AND
EVERYTHING ELSE IS TO
YOUR MIND. WE OURSELVES
ARE IN GOOD HEALTH. I
HAVE OFTEN WRITTEN TO   *Preview of issues*
YOU TO COME AND
INTRODUCE ME, IN ORDER
THAT I MAY BE RELIEVED
FROM MY PRESENT
OCCUPATION. AND NOW IF
IT IS POSSIBLE, AND NONE
OF YOUR WORK HINDERS
YOU, DO TRY AND COME TO
THE ARSINOE FESTIVAL ;
FOR, IF YOU COME, I AM
SURE THAT I SHALL EASILY
BE INTRODUCED TO THE
KING.
(George Milligan, Selections from the Greek Papyri, No. 3. Cambridge University Press, 1912)

Slavery in Scripture
The New Testament does not directly condemn or endorse the institution of slavery. It treats the issue as a fact of life within a fallen world and so provides instructions for living within this system in a manner that honors God. It directs attention toward the higher calling of living for God despite the injustices and sufferings of life. Consider:
- 1 Corinthians 7:20–24
- Ephesians 6:5–9
- Colossians 3:22–4:1
- Philemon 1:1–25

The New Testament also makes it clear that all people are equal before God (1 Corinthians 12:13; Colossians 3:11; Galatians 3:28).

50	60	70	80	90	100 A.D.

49? Jerusalem Council

50–52? Second Missionary Journey by Paul

60–62? Paul arrives in Rome under house arrest

64 Fire in Rome

70 Temple is destroyed

79 Pompeii and Herculaneum are destroyed by Vesuvius eruption

John writes Revelation 95–96?

Church Leadership?

What the apostle Paul writes in his letters concerning overseers and deacons informs us concerning the leadership structure in the New Testament church. In Philippians, Paul singles them out as two distinct groups who exercised some sort of responsibility over other believers in the fellowship. Paul gives further instructions concerning these distinct roles in 1 Timothy 3:1–7 and Titus 1:6–7. There the overlap in the description of an overseer and an elder indicates they are interchangeable terms. That is to say, Paul speaks of two not three leadership roles in the church.

Began and Complete

In Galatians Paul rebukes believers for acting as if they could enter a relationship with God through faith in Christ only to then live as if their progress depended on them rather than God:

> "Are you so foolish? Although you began with the Spirit, are you now trying to finish [or perfect] by human effort?"
>
> Galatians 3:3

The language he uses here to describe the Christian life is exactly the same as he uses in Philippians 1:6 to make the same point: God begins and perfects his work in a believer. Salvation belongs to God from beginning to end.

shock his Christian readers but models the attitude he will develop later in the letter: humility. Paul considers it an honor, not a shame to be a slave because he is a slave of Christ Jesus, the Lord of all.

What is the explanation?

Paul introduces the letter to the church at Philippi by identifying (1–2) himself as the author and noting the company of his dear protégé Timothy. The recipients are identified generally *as all the believers who are in Philippi* but particular mention is made of the leadership of the church who are presumably singled out as the ones responsible for collecting and sending the gift from the church to Paul. The apostle Christianizes a common greeting to declare a blessing that is true for all believers: *God grants us grace that gives us peace with him!*

Two things require our special attention in this introduction in light of the direction the letter takes. First, Paul startlingly labels himself and Timothy as slaves. In a letter where Paul calls believers to imitate others to live as heavenly citizens, it is no mistake that he begins by personally modeling the extent of humility the Philippians are to embrace. Regardless of what society thinks of this lowly status, being a slave of Christ Jesus is an honor. Second, believers are saints whose identities are primarily found in Christ Jesus and only secondarily in their home geographical region. We would do well to remember this: *our identity in Christ precedes that of any flag or nation.*[1]

When Paul thought of the Philippians, he thanked God. Distance, (3–8) current circumstances, and the passing of the years did not lessen his love and appreciation for them. The apostle wanted them to know this up front so that the remainder of the letter springs from love. In these verses, we see how grateful Paul was to God for the Philippians and how deep his love was for them. He continually prayed for them with joy in his heart because he was thankful to God for them. The text presents three reasons for his gratitude:

1. He thanked God for the Philippians because of their participation in the gospel from the very beginning of their Christian experience. Paul was the first to take the gospel to them and he remembered their complete devotion to Christ.[2] They were not just participants in the gospel in that they believed it, and shared the same faith as Paul, but also in that they were actively involved in proclaiming the gospel both personally in Philippi and through financially supporting Paul. The apostle thanked God for these vibrant Christians.

1. Jeremiah 9:24; 1 Corinthians 1:31; 12:27; Galatians 3:28
2. Acts 16:12–40

| B.C. | 40 | | 30 | | 20 | | 10 | | B.C. 1 | A.D. | | 10 |

42   Battle of Philippi   30   Soldiers colonize Philippi   Birth of Paul   4–6?

27   Caesar Augustus begins rule

22

2. Paul's thankful prayers to God were also due to the Philippians' active involvement in the gospel as an expression of God's work within each of them. The fruit of their faith served as evidence that they were being sanctified. God would continue to transform them by the power of the Spirit until the day they stood before their Lord, Jesus Christ.

3. Finally, Paul was also thankful to God for these believers because he loved them. After all, whether Paul was bound in prison or standing before Caesar presenting and defending the gospel, the Philippians were identified with him as fellow believers and ministry supporters. Paul carried them in his heart. His love for them was such that he was willing to call on God as witness to this fact.[3] God could testify that Paul loved the Philippian believers as Jesus did. That is powerful affection.

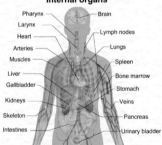

Nikolas Kornilevich Bodarevsky, 1875

The Apostle Paul before Agrippa

Paul affirms his love for the Philippians in light of their identification with him in the events leading up to his current imprisonment in Rome. According to Acts 22–26, these included defending the gospel before the Roman rulers Felix, Festus, and king Agrippa for several years while imprisoned in Caesarea.

(9–11) Paul prays specifically that the Philippians grow in sacrificial love. This love is not just sentimental but also active, for it is based on knowledge and insight of God's truth and its application to life. If the Philippian believers grew in the truth of this love, then they would be able to test what is best and make wise decisions.[4] They would be able to make godly priorities in life and not follow the world. This was important because one day they would stand before Christ.[5] Therefore, Paul desired they live lives that bore visual testimony to the work of Christ in them.[6] This meant being more than just morally pure or sincere. It meant living with righteous and blameless conduct so that others would not stumble. In living like this, God would be praised.

Internal organs

Pharynx — Brain
Larynx
Heart — Lymph nodes
Arteries — Lungs
Muscles — Spleen
Liver — Bone marrow
Gallbladder — Stomach
Kidneys — Veins
Skeleton — Pancreas
Intestines — Urinary bladder

Affection of Christ

The word *affection* is a term that literally means "inside organs" but was used as a figure of speech for the emotions. The ancients associated nobler organs like the heart, liver, and lungs with love and compassion. Paul is emphasizing his love for the Philippians in the most passionate way possible. Not just in the use of the term but also in that his love is like that of Christ.

Partnership in the gospel

Paul thanked God for the Philippian believers' partnership in the gospel (1:5) and because they were joint-partners in God's grace (1:7). The term he uses in both cases is often translated *fellowship*. It simply means *to have something in common*, but Paul means much more than a nice conversation or meal together. *Fellowship* speaks of sharing a common faith and refers to the depth of involvement in one another's lives because of this mutual faith. Because the Philippians shared the same faith as Paul they gave financially to the ministry of the gospel. They were actively involved in God's work by giving to God and not to an individual. Fellowship in giving is just one of many practical expressions of fellowship in faith. Are you a partner in the gospel?

---

3. Romans 1:9; 2 Corinthians 1:23; 1 Thessalonians 2:5, 10
4. Romans 12:2
5. 1 Corinthians 1:8
6. Galatians 5:22–23; Romans 6:13; James 3:18

| 20 | 30 | 40 | 50 | 60 | 70 | A.D. |

Jesus is crucified and resurrected 30–33?

Paul encounters Christ on Damascus road 33–34?

Paul's First Missionary Journey 46–47?

Paul's Second Missionary Journey 50–52?

Paul's Caesarea imprisonment 58–60?

Paul's first Roman imprisonment 60–62?

Paul's second Roman imprisonment and death 67?

What is God saying?

In these introductory words to the Philippians, God speaks to all believers. He challenges Christians concerning the level of gratitude and love they exhibit toward other believers whom he has placed in their lives. Christian divisiveness would be dispelled if believers were to have Paul's attitude of thankfulness toward one another, which characterized his life.[1] God wants Christians to imitate Paul in joyfully and prayerfully thanking him for other believers rather than complaining and resenting them. Believers are to love one another as Christ loves his people, which is a stance that includes an attitude of humility toward others as a slave of Christ.

Where else is this taught in Scripture?

Galatians 5:22–23

But the fruit of the Spirit is love, joy, peace, patience, kindness, goodness, faithfulness, gentleness, and self-control. Against such things there is no law.

Paul's gratitude and prayer in Philippians 1:1–11 concerns the work of sanctification that God is performing in the lives of believers. When God is at work in the life of a submissive believer, attitude and conduct will change resulting in a certain lifestyle. Galatians 5:22–23 sheds light on this issue of the Christian life using the analogy of fruit as well. Galatians 5 concerns sanctification—growing in holiness in the Christian life. The fruit presented is only produced when a believer lives or is led by the Spirit as stated in Galatians 5:16, 18, 25. That is, when he or she yields to the work of the Holy Spirit in his or her life. John 15:4–5, and verse 8 also inform us on this issue through the words of the Lord Jesus Christ. The context in John 15 concerns the maturity of the believer and not his eternal security. Such maturity is a growth that occurs in a believer only when he or she is abiding in Christ.

So the love and joy Paul displays in Philippians 1:1–11 are the first two elements presented in Galatians 5:22–23 as part of the fruit of the Spirit. Paul is an example of a life in the process of being sanctified. Agape love is the first fruit of the Spirit mentioned in Galatians 5. Not only is it the type of love

John 15:4–5

Abide in me and I will abide in you. As the branch cannot bear fruit by itself unless it abides in the vine, so neither can you, unless you abide in me. I am the vine; you are the branches. Whoever abides in me and I in him will produce much fruit for apart from me you can do nothing.

God has demonstrated in Christ toward humanity but is also the love he desires believers to exhibit both toward him, and also other people. In John 15–17, joy is the experience of a life in fellowship with Christ. And so it is clearly God's desire that believers produce fruit so that he may be praised.

Jesus' Imagery of the Vine
John 15 records Jesus' timeless teaching on being connected to the vine in order to bear fruit.

1.   Colossians 1:3–11; 1 Thessalonians 1:2–7; 2 Thessalonians 1:3–4

This passage previews issues that will resurface later in the letter and highlights matters that the apostle addresses elsewhere in Scripture. These concerns are important to God who wants his people to display a certain attitude and conduct in life as his representatives.[2] Christians have a responsibility to serve in different ways using the spiritual gifts which God has granted each believer. Stewardship of our lives will be rendered to and rewarded by God.[3] Moreover, Jesus commanded mutual love among Christians, a love that is exemplified here by Paul, so that the world would know that we are his followers.[4] It is God's will that Christians grow in Christ-likeness.[5] Therefore in this passage, God introduces issues that are clearly important to him.

Agape Love

Greek had several terms for *love* depending on the context:
- *philia*— love among friends
- *eros*—romantic love
- *storge*—family love
- *agape*—self-sacrificial or unconditional love

Paul prays *agape love* or God's love in action, will grow in the lives of believers.
(Deuteronomy 7:7; John 3:16)

Where else does this happen in history?

In 1892 John Nelson Hyde set off from his home in the United States for the Punjab region of India. Hyde had grown up in a Christian home and gone on to attend a Christian Seminary to prepare for ministry. While there, his older brother, who had also given his life to Christian service, died causing Hyde much distress and heart-wrenching reflection about his future. God moved his heart toward the lost in Punjab and Hyde did not hesitate to respond.

The first few years were extremely difficult for him. Hyde struggled with learning the language of the people and was partially deaf. He was present and willing to serve Christ but felt unable. This drove him to his knees in prayer before God. Prayer became Hyde's ministry to the Punjab. He became known as "*Praying Hyde*." He would spend entire nights on his knees or prostrate on the floor before God interceding for people to come to know Christ. This was his passion: to pray that lost people would turn to Jesus. Hyde eventually formed the Punjab Prayer Union that met for prayer for half an hour every day during an annual convention. In the 1908 convention he challenged those present to pray for a conversion to Christ every day of the next year. 400 people trusted in Christ that year. At the 1909 convention, he doubled the challenge to two a day which also happened. At the convention in 1910 he challenged all there to pray that God would save four a day in the incoming year, "Give me souls, Oh God, or I die!" Hyde was known to be unable to eat or sleep with a heavy heart on days he had not heard of multiple conversions to Christ. He ended up ministering across India until late in 1911 when, due to illness, he returned to Chicago. Hyde died a few months later as a result of heart problems. He had been moved with compassion for the glory of God in the salvation of the Punjab people. Like Paul, Hyde's ministry of prayer fueled by love immeasurably impacted India.

John Nelson Hyde
November 9, 1865 to February 17, 1912

Luke 6:12
During this time, Jesus went out to the mountain to pray and spent the night in prayer to God.

2. Ephesians 4:1–6; 1 Peter 4:1; 1 John 1:6–7
3. 1 Corinthians 3:5–9; 12:4–27; 2 Corinthians 5:10
4. John 13:34–35; 1 John 3:11–24
5. Galatians 5:16–25; Ephesians 4:22–24

What does God want?

Through Paul's words, God speaks to us in these verses of Philippians. Now that we have explored the text, we are ready to draw some principles of application. Here are a few important points to consider that emerge from our study. Be intentional about customizing their application to your situation.

Practical Christian living displays God's work in and through you

Paul's gratitude to God for the Philippian Christians was the result of their demonstration of God's work in their lives. They were *active* Christians. This was good because Paul knew they would one day see God face to face. They were showing fruit of God's work within their lives—signs that would result in eternal reward. All believers are slaves of Christ and will one day come before him, including you. Yet, not all Christians humbly seek to serve God in practical ways. We are quick to express outwardly our support for our local sports team, ethnic background, or national identity. However, it seems like we are less eager to get involved in God's interests. Our primary identity as Christians is as slaves of Christ. Our relation to him supersedes all other loyalties. The Philippians gave financially. Others give their talents and time. How do you serve God, or do you? May future reward be part of the motivation you need to live out your faith in practical ways.

The content of your prayers exposes the craving of your heart

What do you pray for? Are your prayers primarily self-serving or are they directed toward the concerns of others? Are they always just a rehashing of your personal wish list or voicing dreams for more stuff? Paul's prayer for the Philippians exposed his heart. His prayers laid bare his passions. He wanted Christians to grow in Christ and he wanted Christ's praise to grow. There is nothing wrong with praying for your own needs and desires, but if that is all you ever pray for, there is a lack of balance that must be corrected. In addition, when you begin to pray more for others and the work of Christ in the world, you may be surprised at how your heart's desires begin to change more towards others and less towards yourself.

Discoveries

Now that you have completed your first excavation into the rich soil of Philippians, it is time to consider what you have learned. Choose the questions that are most helpful to you or your group.

Connecting with the community

These group questions are designed to help you apply what God wants from you. When applicable, think of these questions not only as an individual but also in terms of your family, your community, your nation, and your church.

1.　Paul identifies himself as a slave of Christ. Read the four passages listed in the slavery sidebar on page 21. What does the Bible say? How are you, your family, and your church going to live like slaves of Christ?

2.　In Philippians 1:3–8, the apostle gave three reasons why he was grateful to God for the Philippian believers. What group of believers can you thank God for, using the same three reasons that Paul did?

3.　Philippians 1:6 is a treasured verse to many believers. Discuss how Paul's gratitude described in verses 4–5 relates to his attitude and assurance of the message of verse 6.

4.　Consider the words of Paul's prayer on behalf of the Philippians in verses 9–11. What is it that Paul desires more than anything for the Philippians? What does this tell you about the will of God for his children? How are Paul's requests related to the person and work of Jesus?

5.　Along with Paul, the Bible provides many other examples of prayer warriors whose prayers were geared toward the glory and praise of God. Look at the prayers of Moses (Exodus 32:11–13), Elijah (1 Kings 18:36–37), Hezekiah (2 Kings 19:15–19), and Daniel (Daniel 9:1–19). Discuss the common themes from these prayers and how these ideas will reshape your own prayers.

6. Why is joy so crucial to the message of this letter? What things or circumstances in life affect your joy and why? What can you do to live with joy and pray with joy as Paul does?

7. Look up the references cited in the three sidebar notes on page 19. What is the biblical concept of justification, sanctification, and glorification? How are they different? How are they related? How is God perfecting your Christian walk?

8. In our explanation of Philippians 1:1–11, we affirm that the desire of the apostle Paul was that the Philippians could learn to love sacrificially. Describe this idea of *self-sacrificial love*. What is it that makes it *self-sacrificial*? Could you give some examples of this in action? Does everyone in your group agree on their understanding of self-sacrificial love? What do you have in common? What things do you see differently?

9. How can our understanding and expectation of the "day of Christ" help us in our pursuit of a Christ-like self-sacrificial lifestyle? What practical things can you do as an expression of self-sacrificial love in your community or abroad?

10. How can you as an individual, family, or church display God's love and truth to the community around you this week? What can you intentionally do that demonstrates your enslavement to Christ?

Probing deeper

These research exercises are for your continued study of Philippians in connecting key ideas with other Scripture. They require you to look at other passages beyond the text of Philippians and need to be thought of in terms of yourself, your family, your community, your nation, and your church.

1. Read the introduction to three other epistles by Paul in Ephesians 1:1–3, Galatians 1:1–3, and Colossians 1:1–8. Can you see a difference when you compare them to the introduction of Philippians? Why is this difference important?

2. How is the message of Philippians 1:1–11 related to the message Paul wrote to the church of Corinth in 1 Corinthians 3:5–9; 12:4–27?

3. Read John 13:34–35 and 1 John 3:11–24. How is this text helpful to illuminate the love Paul has for the Philippians and that which he wants them to express? How can you manifest this same kind of love in the midst of your community?

Bringing the story to life

We are called to display God's work in and through our lives. This week, find a way to serve a believer or church with self-sacrificial love just as Paul did with the Philippians. While it is always good to minister to unbelievers, for this assignment it needs to be a believer or church that is served. In Galatians 6:10 Paul states, "so then, as we have opportunity, let us do good to all people, especially to those who are of the household of faith." This could be a group project, church project, or something done by yourself. It may involve one of the following:

- Make or bring a gift to some person or group in need

- Offer to baby-sit to provide a break for a struggling parent

- Fix or repair something for someone

- Provide food for those without or those struggling

- Visit someone who is sick or ill

- Visit someone who is incarcerated

- Take on a clean up project for the church

- Faithfully pray everyday for a month for a particular need or burden of an individual believer or church

The key to this exercise is not merely to love self-sacrificially. It is to respond with joy in the sacrifice made as Paul did. The way in which you serve must come out of love and produce joy for the kingdom work accomplished.

Memorizing the key

Commit to memory the key phrase for Philippians 1:1–11, which is:

Praise God, he is still at work!

Part of learning the Bible is remembering what the Bible is about and where to find things. Memorizing the key phrases will help you to better understand and apply the key points of each book.

Notes, Observations & Questions

Observation journaling

This section will prepare you for *Field Study 3*. You will read Philippians 1:12–26. We have included three types of exercises: some for before you read, some for while you are reading, and some for after you have completed the reading.

Before you read

What are three questions that you would like to ask from the first eleven verses of Philippians? Review Philippians 1:1–11 and write down questions that you hope Paul will explain or expand upon later in the letter. Your questions may include who, what, where, when, why or how. By writing questions, you prepare to engage with what you are about to read.

Question #1:

Question #2:

Question #3:

While you are reading

On the following page, the biblical text is laid out with a wide margin so you can mark the text with questions, key terms, notes, and structures. The verse markings have been removed so you can read it without distractions and have laid out the text with some spacing to help you see how the lines are related. Review the guidelines on *The art of active learning* section, page xi at the beginning of your *Field Notes* for some suggestions on reading, learning, and marking the text effectively.

. Philippians 1:12–26

I want you to know, brothers, that my situation has really turned out for the advance of the gospel, so that it has become known throughout the whole imperial guard and to all the rest that I am in chains for Christ. Most of the brothers having become confident in the Lord because of my chains, are much more bold now to speak the word without fear. Some, to be sure, are preaching Christ from envy and rivalry, but others out of good will. The latter do so out of love because they know that I am put here for the defense of the gospel. The former proclaim Christ out of selfish ambition, not sincerely, supposing they can cause trouble for me in my imprisonment. But what does it matter? Only that in every way, whether in pretense or in truth, Christ is proclaimed. And because of this I rejoice.

Yes, and I will continue to rejoice, for I know that this will turn out for my deliverance through your prayers and the help of the Spirit of Jesus Christ. I confidently hope that I will in no way be ashamed, but that with all boldness, even now as always, Christ will be exalted in my body, whether by life or death. For to me to live is Christ, and to die is gain. Now if I am to go on living in the body, this will mean fruitful labor for me, yet I don't know what I prefer: I am torn between the two. My desire is to depart to be with Christ, for that is far better, but it is more vital on your account to remain in the body. Convinced of this, I know that I will remain and continue with you all for your progress and joy in the faith, so that your boasting may increase in Christ Jesus because of me through my coming to you again.

Notes, Observations & Questions

Summarize the text here

31

After you have read

1. Go back and look at the questions you wrote down from the *before you read* exercise. Did the text answer any of your questions?

2. Write Philippians 1:12–26 from the previous page or your own Bible into a journal word for word. This practice will help you to remember and understand what you have just read. This week, journal your thoughts as you consider what who you should be grateful to God for in your own life.

3. Now read Philippians 1:12–26 in your own Bible. Continue to reread it each day until you get to *Field Study 3*. This will reinforce the learning of Scripture and help you to better retain its message.

Pray

As we learn the Word of God, it is essential that we communicate with him through prayer. Commit to praying throughout the week alone or with others, asking God to help you display him in the world around you. Write your own prayer or use this as a sample prayer:

Dear Father and God,

I come before you today with praise for your holiness and your mercy upon me, a sinner. Thank you for giving me an everlasting love and salvation through your Son. Thank you for reminding me in your word to be grateful for the people you have placed in my life. Forgive me for often complaining about them or taking them for granted. Help me develop a heart of gratitude and love for your people like the apostle Paul possessed. After all, you love them and me unconditionally and sacrificially. Show me how to love others well in practical service to them, utilizing all the gifts and talents you have given me. Everything I am is yours to begin with. Teach me to pray too, Lord. I realize your glory and your praise is more important than getting what I want. Your thoughts and your ways are higher than mine in my limited understanding of the world. May your kingdom be furthered on the earth through the power of your Holy Spirit working in the church. I join with Moses, Paul, and John Hyde in praying that your glory shine through the work of your people. Amen.

Excavate the Site
Philippians 1:12–26
Christ must advance despite hardship

Philippians 1:12–26
FIELD STUDY 3

How is the text arranged?

In the opening of Philippians, Paul challenged us with his deep feelings for other believers. He loved the Philippians and was thankful to God for them and writes to guide them in how to live for Christ in a corrupt society. The apostle uses his own imprisonment as a mirror to help the Philippians see how to respond to their own persecution. Read the biblical text several times reflecting upon Paul's situation. See also if you can identify how his thoughts unfold before looking at the guide provided:

Philippians 1:12–26

Section	Bible Text
Present Situation: Chains (1:12–18b)	
The gospel spreads throughout the palace	¹² I want you to know, brothers, that my situation has really turned out for the advance of the gospel, ¹³ so that it has become known throughout the whole imperial guard and to all the rest that I am in chains for Christ.
The gospel spreads throughout the town	¹⁴ Most of the brothers having become confident in the Lord because of my chains, are much more bold now to speak the word without fear. ¹⁵ Some, to be sure, are preaching Christ from envy and rivalry, but others out of good will. ¹⁶ The latter do so out of love because they know that I am put here for the defense of the gospel.

Rembrandt Harmenszoon van Rijn, 1627

The Apostle Paul in Prison
Paul's house arrest in Rome served to further the gospel long beyond the apostle's lifespan. The letters that he wrote under the inspiration of the Holy Spirit continue to serve the church today as part of the canon of Scripture.

Philippians 1:12–26

Section	Bible Text
The gospel spreads throughout the town (continued)	[17] The former proclaim Christ out of selfish ambition, not sincerely, supposing they can cause trouble for me in my imprisonment. [18a] But what does it matter? Only that in every way, whether in pretense or in truth, Christ is proclaimed.
Paul's current response: Joy	[18b] And because of this I rejoice.
Future Situation: Freedom (1:18c–26)	
Paul's ongoing response: Joy	[18c] Yes, and I will continue to rejoice,
Paul's confidence of release	[19] for I know that this will turn out for my deliverance through your prayers and the help of the Spirit of Jesus Christ. [20] I confidently hope that I will in no way be ashamed, but that with all boldness, even now as always, Christ will be exalted in my body, whether by life or death.
Paul's passion to magnify Christ	[21] For to me to live is Christ, and to die is gain. [22] Now if I am to go on living in the body, this will mean fruitful labor for me, yet I don't know what I prefer: [23] I am torn between the two. My desire is to depart to be with Christ, for that is far better, [24] but it is more vital on your account to remain in the body.
Anticipation of release	[25] Convinced of this, I know that I will remain and continue with you all for your progress and joy in the faith, [26] so that your boasting may increase in Christ Jesus because of me through my coming to you again.

As you can see from the outline, the broad content of this passage is divided between Paul's present and future situation. At the core of the passage, is an attitude of joy. Let's continue to dig through the text together.

What is this passage saying?

What are some key terms and phrases?

Here are some key terms, phrases, and concepts useful to understanding this passage. They will prepare you for grasping the explanation section that follows.

Emphasis on Joy

Have you noticed how Paul's sentiments in the opening chapter of this letter have been saturated with joy? Look at how Paul:
- Prays with joy (1:4)
- Rejoices regarding his current situation (1:18a)
- Continues to rejoice concerning what is ahead (1:18b)
- Desires the Philippians have joy in the faith (1:25)

Joy is an integral Christian trait.

Meaning of Key Terms

Key word or phrase	Meaning and significance
For the *advance* of the gospel… your *progress* and joy in the faith (1:12, 25)	Paul uses the same word to describe two important points. Translated as *advance* in verse 12 and *progress* in verse 25, it is important to note that they are the same word. The term simply means *forward movement to an improved state* and takes on great significance in the contexts Paul uses. It was also a term used to describe the activity of army engineers who pioneered the advance of a military unit tracking behind. Paul was a pioneering missionary who took the gospel to Philippi and now this gospel was advancing into new spheres of influence in Rome. Paul's first use of *advance* is in the context of *pioneering evangelism*. The second use, translated *progress*, concerns the *progress of the Philippian believers in the faith*. Paul is confident his release will enable him to be a part of these believers' movement into new spheres of sanctification. Therefore, Paul's second use of the same term is in the context of *discipleship*. Despite his arrest, evangelism was being accomplished as the gospel message was reaching new people, bringing glory to Christ and joy to Paul. Discipleship or the outworking of the gospel in the lives of those who believed it, made Paul rejoice, and was reason to boast in Christ. The advance of the gospel and progress of believers in the faith are simply ways of talking about evangelism and discipleship.
Deliverance (1:19)	The term deliverance can also be translated as *salvation*. What was the deliverance Paul anticipated? Was it the release from house arrest? Was it the vindication of his person, beliefs, and ministry before the Roman authorities? Was it his ultimate salvation before God? It appears that when Paul mentions "this" in verse 19, he has in mind his entire situation. It includes everything from his unfair arrest in Jerusalem up to and including his house arrest in Rome (Acts 22–28). Also included would be the consequences of his imprisonment described in verses 12–18 as *the advance of the gospel*. Verses 25–26 indicate Paul was confident he would be released from house arrest. It is likely that physical release was also part of the deliverance he expected. Paul's words echoing Job 13:16 where Job expects vindication from God to whom he pleads his case, given his suffering. In doing so, Paul recasts Job's situation as his own. After all, the broader situation Paul faced was a tribunal before the Roman authorities where he and the message he proclaimed were under investigation. Job too was seeking vindication from God using tribunal language. Therefore, Paul was confident that God would vindicate him through the work of the Holy Spirit and the prayers of other believers, and this would result in his release.

Trajan's Bridge over the Danube

Apollodorus of Damascus was the army engineer who constructed Trajan's bridge over the Danube. It allowed the Roman Emperor Trajan to "make progress" with his armies across the lower Danube in the second war against the Dacia ultimately bringing victory to the Roman Empire and illustrates Paul's use of the word *progress*.

Evangelism

Evangelism is the spread of the Christian gospel message to those who have not heard it or believed it. This was part of Paul's mission as he traveled from place to place, preaching the gospel and establishing churches throughout the Roman Empire.

Discipleship

Discipleship is the modeling of one's life as a follower of Jesus to grow in Christlikeness. It is also known as the process of sanctification. Paul's continual encouragement, exhortations, rebukes, and training of his churches were part of their discipleship process.

Job 13:16

This will be my deliverance, for no godless individual would stand before him.

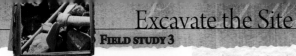
Who were the Judaizers?

Judaizers were those in the early church seeking to enforce the requirements of a Jewish lifestyle, particularly adherence to the Law of Moses and the rite of circumcision, upon Christians. They were predominantly Christians who did not understand the practical implications of the death and resurrection of Jesus Christ, which brought about the new age of the church. These are probably the types of people Paul warns about in Philippians 3.

Romans 14:1–4

Receive the weak in faith but not to dispute over opinions. One believes he may eat everything but he who is weak eats only vegetables. The one who eats everything should not despise the one who does not, and the one who does not eat everything should not pass judgment on the one who does, for God has accepted him. Who are you to judge another one's servant? Before his own master he stands or falls. And he will stand, for the Lord is able to make him stand.

A Future Day of Christ

In Philippians 1:6 Paul discussed a time in every believer's future when he or she will directly encounter Jesus Christ. Faithfulness and service to God will be exposed and rewarded accordingly. This is what motivated and shaped Paul's life.

Meaning of Key Terms

Key word or phrase	Meaning and significance
Preaching Christ from envy and rivalry... (1:15) ...cause trouble for me (1:17)	Who were these opponents of Paul mentioned in verses 15–17? It is possible that these people were unbelievers who were trying to tarnish the Christian faith in order to make life hard for the apostle. However, it is more likely these opponents were actually Christians. This may come as a bit of a surprise to us, but the immediate context indicates that these opponents were present in Rome, where Paul was under house arrest. Moreover, verses 15–17 come as a clarification of the statement in verse 14, where believers were emboldened to proclaim Christ given Paul's chains. Paul is presenting two distinct motivations believers may have in their proclamation of the gospel. In addition, the apostle does not question the truth of the gospel they preach, only their motivation behind their proclamation. These opponents seem to be Christians in Rome. They may have been opportunists within the church who saw Paul's confinement as creating room for their rise into influence or power. They also may have been believers sulking over Paul's words to them some years earlier recorded in Romans 14:1–4, 10–12. They may have been Christians who disagreed with Paul's theology in some way—maybe even Judaizing Christians—that saw Paul's chains as God's disciplinary restraint. As difficult as it must have been for Paul to accept such unfair opposition from believers, his response towards them is also surprising. Yet, his understanding regarding accountability on the Day of Christ Jesus may have helped him develop this attitude. He rejoices that God's truth advances despite the imperfect motives of the messengers. What matters most is that Christ is proclaimed.

What about the culture?

In Philippians 1:12–26, Paul presents his current situation to the church at Philippi. Ancient letters often began with information on the sender's situation just as personal letters do today. Look at how the author of the ancient letter below parallels what Paul is doing in Philippians albeit in fewer words. Apollinarius was a soldier writing to his mother Taesis in the second century A.D. He is requesting that she not worry because he safely arrived in Rome though he is to be posted to Misemum. Note how his letter also contains the same conventions of letter writing which we previously examined:

> Apollinarius to Taesis, his mother and lady, many greetings.
> Before all else I pray for your health. I myself am well, and I make deferential respect on your behalf before the gods of this place.

B.C.	1	A.D.	10		20		30		40		50

5? Birth of Jesus		John the Baptist begins his ministry 28–29?		33–34? Paul encounters Christ on Damascus road	46–47? First Missionary
	4–6? Birth of Paul	Jesus begins his ministry 28–30?			Journey by Pau
		Jesus is crucified and resurrected 30–33?			

I wish you to know, mother, that I arrived in Rome in good health on the 25th of the month Pachon and was assigned to Misenum when I wrote you this letter. But I have not yet learned my century, for I have not gone to Misenum when I wrote you this letter. I beg you then, mother, take care of yourself, and do not worry about me, for I have come into a fine place…"

It is also important to understand a little about the Imperial Guard to see the extent of the progress that the gospel was making among Caesar's closest staff because of Paul's imprisonment. The Praetorian Guard was an elite unit of soldiers responsible for protecting the emperor. These bodyguards were well trained, well paid, and well looked after. They were offered good retirement plans to ensure their loyalty, and they came to hold great military and political power. Their proximity to the emperor gave them many opportunities to depose a Caesar and install another, which did happen on occasion. Aside from guarding and patrolling the palaces, and protecting the emperor and his interests, they also had other responsibilities such as watching over individuals like Paul who were awaiting an audience with Caesar. Guards would have been chained to Paul at the wrist on four-hour shifts around the clock allowing him to write and meet visitors but making sure he remained under house arrest. This meant that many soldiers were forced to spend uninterrupted time with the apostle.

The Roman emperor at this time was Nero, who became a very unpopular ruler because of his cruel and perverted interests. His unpopularity among important members of the Praetorian Guard was no secret. According to the Roman historian Tacitus, Subrius Flavius was a high-ranking soldier involved in a failed attempt to overthrow Nero in A.D. 65. Tacitus writes that when the soldier was questioned by Nero as to why he had abandoned his oath of allegiance, the soldier replied:

I abhorred you… though there was not a soldier in the whole army more loyal to you than I so long as you deserved to be loved; but I began to hate you when you

Praetorian Guard

The Praetorian Guard was an elite force of body guards, initially composed of about 9,000 soldiers although the number varied from emperor to emperor. They became prominent around 275 B.C. and remained a dominant force until they were dissolved by Constantine in the 4th century A.D.

Nero's Torches

Nero was the Roman Emperor from A.D. 54 to 68. After the great fire in Rome in A.D. 64 which he himself may have ordered to expand his palaces, he brutally and savagely persecuted Christians as scapegoats for the fire. Torture included being burned alive as a human torch.

Henryk Siemiradzki, 1876

49? Jerusalem Council

50–52? Second Missionary Journey by Paul

60–62? Paul arrives in Rome under house arrest

64 Fire in Rome

70 Temple is destroyed

79 Pompeii and Herculaneum are destroyed by Vesuvius eruption

John writes Revelation 95–96?

Paul's Present Situation

Paul's current situation of imprisonment is but the climax of several years of difficulty in chains. He was arrested in Jerusalem, spent time in Caesarea, and now was in Rome. The situation surrounding this bondage had involved much more than imprisonment. He had also been attacked by a mob, survived a murder plot, a sea storm, and a snake bite. These were all part of the imprisoned situation in which Paul rejoiced because it allowed the gospel to advance (Acts 22–28).

became the murderer of your mother and wife, a charioteer, an actor, and an incendiary.

(Tacitus Annals 15.67)

Eventually, the Praetorian Guard abandoned Nero. Paul's chains created a link between the gospel and influential soldiers in the administration of the empire. The most loyal of Roman soldiers were turning to Christ.

What is the explanation?

We are now ready to dig a little deeper into the text and examine more closely how Paul uses his difficult situation as a platform from which to guide the Philippian believers.

The Roman historian Tacitus

Tacitus (A.D. 56–117) was a Roman historian and senator who wrote a history of the Roman Empire. His two main works, *the Annals* and *the Histories*, examine several emperors including Nero, providing a reliable understanding of events relevant to the time period in which Philippians was written.

The Present situation: The Philippian believers were concerned for Paul and his hardships. Their financial help was an overflow of their commitment to God as well as their love for the apostle. Therefore, Paul sends them this letter in order to shape their mindset about their present situation by using insights from his. He viewed his present bondage as an occasion for joy because Christ was being proclaimed into new areas. Paul's difficult situation was no accident. Slaves of Christ are not immune from hardship. God allowed Paul to do what Paul longed to do and more. He was not just preaching in Rome. He was now witnessing to Rome's elite. Even though his chains prevented him from preaching at the market, they guaranteed an audience at the palace with the rulers of the Empire. Attempts to silence him and suppress the gospel were having the opposite effect.

So how was the gospel moving freely into new areas despite Paul's captivity? Paul mentions two ways in which it was spreading. The first was through his own ministry to Caesar's immediate staff. Caesar's most loyal troops and administrators were hearing of a Lord greater than Caesar! They came to know that Paul was in chains because of his faith and not for committing a crime. Paul viewed his imprisoned situation as an opportunity to share the gospel with them. Chains could not restrain his tongue.

The second way in which the gospel was spreading was through the

The Spirit of Jesus Christ

In verse 19, *the Spirit of Jesus Christ* is a reference to the Holy Spirit—the third member of the Trinity. Paul can refer to the Holy Spirit here as the Spirit of Jesus Christ because Jesus declared that he would send the Holy Spirit to aid his followers in his absence (John 15:26; 16:7). Paul is not saying that the Holy Spirit is not a distinct person in the Trinity or just some kind of life-force of Jesus Christ. He is simply referring to the Holy Spirit as the one who supplies the believer with the living presence of Christ in this age in history.

B.C.	40		30		20		10		B.C. 1	A.D.		10

42 Battle of Philippi | 30 Soldiers colonize Philippi   Birth of Paul   4–6?

                 | 27 Caesar Augustus begins rule

Christians in Rome. Paul was thrilled that believers were mobilized by his captivity even though some had different motivations. While some were opponents, others saw Paul's circumstances as a rallying call for them to stand up and be counted for their faith. Undoubtedly, they saw his situation as an appointment set up by God for the gospel to go to the rulers of the Empire. Therefore, it was their responsibility to spread the gospel across town. And so, some preached Christ as though ministry were a competition in which one could outperform another. Others however, saw it as a team effort. Ultimately, what was important to Paul was that the gospel continued to spread across the Empire in spite of, and because of his situation. The proclamation of Christ was all that mattered and is what filled Paul with joy.

(16–26) The Future situation: Paul's present situation was not the only occasion for rejoicing. The future filled him with joy too. Paul was confidant his present bondage and impending defense before Caesar would give way to deliverance. He believed God would answer the prayers of the Philippian believers favorably and would grant him the necessary help in his hour of need by the power of the Holy Spirit. Paul knew that God chose to work through the power of the Spirit and the prayers of his people. He was filled with ongoing joy because of his confidence that no matter what the outcome for him, Christ would be magnified. Therefore, Paul's desire—in life or death—was to boldly magnify Jesus and his glorious gospel.

The apostle reflected on the possibilities of life and death. What he says provides an insight into the attitude of this great man of God. Paul's perspective about life and death is a challenge for all believers. His motto in life was to live productively for Christ. He knew he would one-day stand before his Lord. Likewise, he viewed death as a beneficial and necessary passageway into the immediate presence of Christ. And so, Paul was torn. His preference was to die to be with Christ since this was to his advantage. However, his confidence was that he would live to continue to help the Philippian believers grow with joy in Christ to their advantage. Paul expected to live, and through his release, add to the Philippians' boasting in Christ.[1]

Public Domain

1.   Jeremiah 9:23–24

Irony through Wordplay?

There is both irony and a sort of wordplay in what Paul is doing when he uses the term "advance" or "progress" in verse 12. He is informing the Philippians that his captivity has turned out to further the gospel. The clear implication is that the Philippians thought Paul's chains would have the opposite effect and be a hindrance. The irony is that Paul looks at his chains with a smile on his face because they may bind him but not the message of God. There is also a sort of mental wordplay or conceptual spin that emphasizes this as well. Incarceration and chains may make an onlooker think the gospel is hindered when in fact it is advancing. God cannot be chained.

Word Play

Verse 12	**prokopēn** *προκοπην*	=	Advance Furtherance
Verse 25	**proskopēn** *προσκοπην*	=	Obstacle Hindrance

Ignatius, Bishop of Antioch

Ignatius was an early Christian leader who wrote letters of encouragement to churches while on the way to his martyrdom in Rome where he was eaten by lions. To the church in Philadelphia, he states, "their prayers will perfect me." Like Paul, Ignatius understood the power of prayer to accomplish God's will in his own life-threatening trial.

---

20   30   40   50   60   70   A.D.

Jesus is crucified and resurrected 30–33?

Paul's First Missionary Journey 46–47?

Paul's first Roman imprisonment 60–62?

Paul encounters Christ on Damascus road 33–34?

Paul's Caesarea imprisonment 58–60?

Paul's second Roman imprisonment and death 67?

Paul's Second Missionary Journey 50–52?

39

Christian Boasting

The idea of boasting is negative to many of us. It is arrogant and big-headed. But this is only the case if wrongly motivated and directed. Boasting in Christ means expressing our confidence and joy in who he is and what he has done. Jeremiah 9:23–24 declares that we are to boast in the knowledge and understanding of the Lord.

What is God saying?

In this passage, God provides practical advice for daily Christian living. He uses Paul's attitude and response to his imprisonment as a teaching tool for believers. Like Paul, believers are not exempt from difficulty. This is precisely because God uses difficult situations in order to advance his offer of salvation. God sees our difficulties as opportunities to catch the eye of a watching world. How believers cope with unfair criticism, illness, grief, suffering, and persecution makes a clear statement about the depth of our Christian character, our focus, our faith, and our hope in God. This passage illustrates visually what should be the primary focus of the Christian life: to proclaim Christ at all costs with the right attitude. In doing so, it reminds Christians that life must be entirely about advancing and growing in Jesus Christ. Death is not an event to fear, but the passage into eternal life with the Savior.

Where else is this taught in Scripture?

When we consider the narratives in the book of Acts, we observe that the experience of the early New Testament church is comparable to Paul's situation in Philippians 1:12–26. Acts presents the story of the progress of the gospel of salvation in Jesus Christ through believers as they are empowered by the Holy Spirit. Progress is a theme in the story of Acts and can be seen in the many *progress reports* (Acts 2:47; 6:7; 9:31; 12:24; 16:5; 19:20; 28:30–31). This advance of the gospel pioneers into new geographical places and new ethnic people groups. It is the fulfillment of God's will and plan as expressed through Jesus in Acts 1:8. Hardship and persecution are the channels used by God to advance the gospel message to the ends of the earth. This is seen in the broad movements of the overall story as well as in the short stories within. The gospel moves out of Jerusalem and into the surrounding Judean and Samarian regions because of persecution resulting from the death of Stephen. Peter, John, Stephen, Paul, Barnabas, Silas, and the apostles in general with many other unnamed believers are presented as undergoing hardship so that the gospel progresses. Paul views his difficult situation as a testimony to the presence of God's hand moving the events of history as he pleases.

Stoning of Stephen

Stephen's martyrdom in Acts 7–8 pushed the gospel out to Antioch on the Orontes, where a Christian church was formed that launched the missionary journeys of Paul across the known Roman world (Acts 11:19–20).

Here is a particular example of what seems to be an endless list in the Scriptures. God repeatedly allows trials, suffering, and persecution in the lives of his faithful representatives so that they may serve to advance his will and plan in history. Here are a few examples:

- Joseph (*Genesis 50:19–20*)
- Moses (*Numbers 12:1; 14:1–2; 21:5*)
- Elijah (*1 Kings 19:1–18*)
- Shadrach, Meshach, and Abednego (*Daniel 3:16–18, 28–29*)
- Daniel (*Daniel 6:1–28*)
- Jeremiah (*Jeremiah 11:18–23; 26:1–11; 37:14–16; 38:6*)
- John the Baptist (*Matthew 14:3–12*)

Suffering and hardship are God's means of accomplishing his will and plan in history through Jesus.[1] As Christians, it should not surprise us that evangelism and discipleship advance through difficult circumstances for it is in such conditions that the world takes note of what Christians believe (evangelism). Trials and suffering develop the character, attitude, faith, hope in the lives of believers (discipleship), and a desire to boast exclusively in God.

To Die is Gain

Paul's view of death as gain is not a morbid death wish resulting from dissatisfaction with life, nor a means of escaping current hardship. It is the hope of one who truly knows the greatness of what awaits the believer in Jesus. Since Christ lived in Paul, Paul lived for Christ. The end of this life meant entering into something much better: eternal life with Jesus. Because death had lost its sting, Paul knew it was not a threat to be feared by Christians, but a hope to look forward to.

Where else does this happen in history?

Bruce Olson is a modern-day example of godly service in a difficult situation. What is remarkable is that his response has been consistent throughout the decades that his hardships have lasted. Bruce set out alone for the South American jungles between Venezuela and Colombia in the early 1960's because he had been rejected by every missionary agency he had applied to. He was just 19 when he boarded a plane to Venezuela knowing no Spanish and having just a few dollars. What he did possess, however, was a burning passion to tell the unreached Motilone jungle tribes about the love of Jesus. These native people Bruce wanted to reach were violent; they didn't care for their elderly and left orphans out as food for wild beasts. Their treatment of Bruce over the years was brutal and bloody as well. Jungle life was cruel, filled with disease, loneliness, exposure to the elements, kidnapping by guerrilla forces, as well as the expected threat from large animals and deadly insects. On many occasions Bruce faced torture, pain, grief, discouragement, and near death from illness, bullets, and arrows. Decade after decade Bruce endured all sorts of difficulties and hardships out of a love for God and those unreached by the gospel. He still lives for God in this way. Bruce Olson's life reiterates the Apostle Paul's situation in Philippians. Both proclaim that Christ is worth living or dying for. Extreme circumstances can be endured if our focus is fixed on God.

Jungles of Venezuela
Bruce Olson was just 19 years old when he first ventured into the uncharted jungles of Venezuela to reach the Motilone people with the gospel.

1. Mark 8:31; 9:31; 10:33–34; Hebrews 5:7–10

1 Corinthians 15:54–55

When the perishable puts on the imperishable, and the mortal puts on immortality, then the saying that is written will come true, 'Death has been swallowed up in victory. Where, Death, is your victory? Where, Death, is your sting?'

What does God want?

There are many implications for our daily lives that emerge from this passage of Scripture. We will focus on two related to how Paul models the response God wants for us in the midst of persecution and suffering. Remember that God is using Paul's imprisonment to inform both the Philippians and us about how to respond to hardship. God wants you to do something with what he says.

Since Christ lives in you, serve him at all costs with the right attitude

Paul's single goal and passion in life was to magnify Jesus Christ. This is because Christ lived in him. His future hope of being *with* Christ affected his present living *for* Christ. This is the calling of all believers. If Christ lives in you, his desire is that you live for him. You get to serve God, but in a godless society, this is not easy. In fact, it may be costly. You may not be chained as Paul was, but your faith in Jesus will always be put to the test by a world that has no time or place for him. You may already feel disappointed, marginalized, and perhaps picked on for being a Christian. How do you live for Christ? Do you live to know him? Do you live to proclaim him? Is the gospel message advancing through you? Are the implications of believing in the gospel affecting you? Are you willing to suffer for Christ even to the point of death? Paul's response in the midst of his tribulations is an exact model of what God expects from you. Joy and confidence in Christ will prevent you too from becoming bitter under harsh treatment. Paul didn't see his situation as an excuse to moan or be silent. He knew the bigger picture. Better still, he knew his sovereign God. Christ was being served through his hardship and this brought him joy. For Paul, to live was Christ and to die was gain. What do you live for? What would you die for?

How you cope within hard times testifies to your faith

Difficulties are like a filter that orders life's priorities. It is when we are undergoing hardship that we are able to recognize what is truly most important for us in life. Paul's imprisonment caused the Philippians some grief, but he viewed it as God's plan. God ordained Paul's imprisonment. Paul invites us all to watch him cope in a harsh situation and undergo hurt from jealous Christians. Watch and learn. He was so confident in God's love that nothing could shake his faith. Rather, he viewed the everyday details of life as packed with God's providential purpose—even the sufferings. So how do you cope with what is going on in your life today? What does your situation tell you about your relationship with God? How can you use the eyes of faith so that you can see the good, eternal purpose of God even in the most painful and unjust circumstances of life?

Discoveries

Now that you have completed your second excavation into the ancient riches of the book of Philippians, it is time to sift through your *Discoveries* and see what you have learned. Carefully choose the questions that are most helpful to you or your group.

Connecting with the community

These discussion questions will help you apply what God wants from you. When applicable, think of these questions not only as an individual but also in terms of your family, your community, your nation, and your church.

1. Even through suffering, Paul's concern was for the *progress* of the gospel, which included both evangelism and discipleship. What strategies does your local church have in place for evangelism and discipleship? What could be done if believers were willing to suffer for the sake of advancing the gospel? Will you do it?

2. Paul's present situation filled him with joy, as did his future situation. How is that possible in light of his difficult circumstances? How can we model that same attitude?

3. Paul had a unique supernatural experience of the life to come in 2 Corinthians 12:1–4. Read it along with Paul's statements in Galatians 2:20 and 2 Corinthians 5:8. What can we learn from the apostle's experience and attitude?

4. The Bible speaks about death in a variety of ways, which brings comfort to believers. Look up 1 Thessalonians 4:14, 2 Timothy 4:6, and John 14:1–3. How are believers to view death?

5. The apostle Paul affirms that because of his imprisonment, the gospel was being proclaimed more widely. However, not all who preached the gospel had godly intentions. What does this tell you about the reality of Christian ministry in a fallen world?

6. Who were the Judaizers that opposed Paul? What was their message? How did they oppose the truth and joy of the gospel?

7. Consider the role of prayer in verse 19 as God allows us to be a part of the means through which he chooses to operate. Who do you or your church support in prayer for deliverance? Will you faithfully uphold suffering believers in prayer?

8. Paul was not immune from suffering but God used his hardship to further the gospel. How well do we as individuals or churches suffer in front of a watching world? How can we better incarnate the gospel?

9. How are we to handle competition in ministry? What can we learn from Paul's response to those who preached the gospel with ulterior motives?

Probing deeper

These exercises are for your continued study of our Philippians passage by further researching supporting biblical texts. They also need to be thought of in terms of yourself, your family, your community, your nation, and your church.

1. Compare Paul's difficulties in Philippians 1:12–26 with Daniel 4:1–5:31. What role does hardship have in the life of the faithful believer?

2. Paul addresses the issues caused by Judaizers in Galatians. Read Galatians 2:4, 12, 16, 19; 5:1–3 as well as Acts 15:1; 21:20–25. What does Paul teach in relation to the Judaizers? How does a legalistic mindset, similar to the Judaizers affect the church today?

3. Throughout Scripture, we see believers suffer for the advance of God's plan in history. Read the following passages:
   • 2 Timothy 2:8–13
   • Romans 5:3–5
   • Colossians 1:27
   • 1 Corinthians 1:31
   • 2 Corinthians 10:17
   What do these passages teach about suffering and God's purposes? What is God accomplishing through Paul's suffering in Philippians?

4. Read the account of Peter and John in Acts 4:1–33. How can injustice and pain be used as a God-given privilege for the sake of the gospel? What does this teach us about God?

Bringing the story to life

The Apostle Paul was understood to be one of the earliest martyrs of the Church, but persecution of Christians is rampant all over the world today. Yet even in heavy persecution, the Church is unified and grows stronger in Christ. Paul himself rejoiced in his chains:

> "But what does it matter? Only that in every way, whether in pretense or in truth, Christ is proclaimed. And because of this I rejoice. Yes, and I will continue to rejoice, for I know that this will turn out for my deliverance through your prayers and the help of the Spirit of Jesus Christ.."
>
> Philippians 1:18–19

Research a country or region of the world in which Christians are being persecuted today. You may already know of persecution that is happening around you personally. Your pastor or church may have information about persecuted believers around the world. If you have access to the internet, these websites may be helpful:

- www.OperationWorld.org
- www.OpenDoors.org
- www.persecution.org
- www.ChristianFreedom.org
- www.persecution.com

Write down some notes on the number of Christians in the region suffering persecution and their circumstances.

Write a prayer for these Christians that you can use to pray over them every day for a month. As Paul prayed in Philippians, pray not only for their protection and well-being, but that for the hope that the gospel message will be advanced. Thank God that all of this worldly persecution will eventually lead to their deliverance and that God will be glorified through his Son, Jesus Christ. If possible, have others join you in this daily prayer.

Memorizing the key

Commit to memory the key phrase for Philippians 1:12–26, which is:

Christ must advance despite hardship

Part of learning the Bible is remembering what the Bible is about and where to find things. Memorizing the key phrases will help you to better understand and apply the key points of Philippians. Once you have completed the entire study of Philippians, you will be able to recite the main point or purpose of each section of Philippians. These phrases will remind you of the entire argument that Paul is making.

Observation journaling

This section will prepare you for *Field Study 4* by reading through Philippians 1:27–2:4. We have included three types of exercises: some for before you read, some for while you are reading, and some for after you have completed the reading.

Before you read

As believers in Christ, we are destined for eternal life with him. This means that one day we will be citizens of heaven. How should heavenly citizenship affect our actions towards other people? In the space below, write out how our heavenly citizenship should affect our actions toward others.

While you are reading

On the following page, the biblical text is laid out with a wide margin so you can mark the text with questions, key terms, notes, and structures. The verse markings have been removed so you can read it without distractions and have laid out the text with some spacing to help you see how the lines are related. Review the guidelines on *The art of active learning* section, page xi at the beginning of your *Field Notes* for some suggestions on reading, learning, and marking the text effectively.

Philippians 1:27–2:4

Only live as citizens in a manner worthy of the gospel of Christ so that, whether I come and see you or remain absent, I will hear that you are standing firm in one spirit, with one mind, contending side by side for the faith of the gospel, and not being intimidated in any way by your opponents—which is a sign to them of their destruction, but of salvation for you, and that from God. For it has been granted to you on behalf of Christ, not only to believe in him but also to suffer for him, experiencing the same conflict which you saw I had and now hear that I still have.

Therefore, if there is any encouragement in Christ, if any comfort from love, if any fellowship in the Spirit, if any affection and mercy, then complete my joy and be like-minded, by having the same love, united in spirit and purpose. Instead of being motivated by selfish ambition or vain conceit, each of you in humility should consider others more significant than yourselves. Each of you should look out not only for your own interests, but also for the interests of others.

Notes, Observations & Questions

Summarize the text here

Notes, Observations & Questions

After you have read

1. Journaling is another way to help us learn. Write out Philippians 1:27–2:4 from the previous page or your own Bible into a journal word for word. This practice will help you to remember and understand what you have just read. This week, journal your thoughts as you consider what it means to suffer for Christ before a watching world. What is the impact on your own family, community, nation, and church?

2. Now read Philippians 1:27–2:4 in your own Bible. Continue to reread it each day until you get to *Field Study 4*. This will reinforce the learning of Scripture and help you to better retain its message.

Pray

As we learn the word of God, it is essential that we communicate with him through prayer. Consider writing a prayer, psalm, or poem to God. Writing it out will help you reflect on your attitude when going through hardship. Commit to praying throughout the week for your church, family, and yourself and what it means to suffer for Christ. Try to pray with a friend or family member. Consider this as a sample prayer:

Dear Merciful Father,

I praise you for your faithfulness and lifelong love for me. Thank you for teaching me through your holy word and allowing me to see its applications in my own life by the power of the Holy Spirit. I thank you even for the difficulties in my life because I know you are working them out for my good and your glory. Life is often difficult. It's hard to see good coming from the bad times. It is also hard to have the right attitude when I am in the midst of trying circumstances. Father, I realize I am not safe from hardship simply because I am a Christian. Help me develop the mindset you want me to exhibit so that I too can rejoice in what you can do in me and through me in the midst of difficult situations. I know the world watches Christians, always ready to point fingers and highlight our failures. Help us be strong. Help us be people of joy. Help me live to magnify Jesus Christ just like Paul. Help me live for you God. Amen.

Excavate the Site

Philippians 1:27–2:4

FIELD STUDY 4

How is the text arranged?

Philippians 1:27–2:4 marks the beginning of the central section of the epistle. Within it, Paul makes an appeal to the Philippians, which he will sustain through much of the letter. Take some time to read and meditate on this ancient passage, which we will explore together. Check the outline provided as well so you can see the general flow of Paul's thoughts:

Philippians 1:27–2:4

Section	Bible Text
Central Appeal	27 Only live as citizens in a manner worthy of the gospel of Christ

Worthy Christian Walking	so that,
	   whether I come and see you or remain absent,
	   I will hear that you are standing firm in one spirit,
	      with one mind,
	         contending side by side for the faith of the gospel,
	28 and not being intimidated in any way by your opponents
	      —which is a sign to them of their destruction,
	   but of salvation for you, and that from God.
	
	29 For it has been granted to you on behalf of Christ,
	   not only to believe in him but also to suffer for him,
	30 experiencing the same conflict which you saw I had
	   and now hear that I still have.

Unworthy Christian Walking	2:1 Therefore, if there is any encouragement in Christ,
	         if any comfort from love,
	         if any fellowship in the Spirit,
	         if any affection and mercy,

Polycarp's Letter

Polycarp was an early church leader who wrote to the Philippians between 110 and 140 A.D. Believed to be discipled by the Apostle John, Polycarp's letter to the believers in Philippi encouraged a subsequent generation of Christians to also walk worthy of God, stating:

Knowing then that God is not mocked, we ought to walk worthily of his commandment and glory.
   (Letter to the Philippians 5:1)

Philippians 1:27–2:4

Section	Bible Text
Unworthy Christian Walking (*continued*)	² then complete my joy and be like-minded, by having the same love, united in spirit and purpose. ³ Instead of being motivated by selfish ambition or vain conceit, each of you in humility should consider others more significant than yourselves. ⁴ Each of you should look out not only for your own interests, but also for the interests of others.

Philippians 1:27–2:4 is divided into three units. In the first unit, Paul begins by expressing his central appeal concerning Christian living. In the next two sections, he instructs the Philippian believers on how to adhere to such a lifestyle by explaining both how, and how not to live.

What is this passage saying?

What are some key terms and phrases?

Take some time now to study and understand the following key terms, phrases, and concepts. They will be very useful in understanding the meaning and significance of this passage.

Walking with God

Often, the apostle Paul uses the metaphor of a *walk* with respect to a believers relationship with God. This is the case in Romans 13:13; Ephesians 4:1; Galatians 5:16 and 1 Thessalonians 2:12. In Philippians however, Paul uses the metaphor of citizenship to communicate the believers relationship to God because of the high value Philippi placed on Roman citizenship.

Meaning of Key Terms

Key word or phrase	Meaning and significance
Live as citizens (1:27)	This is an extremely important phrase in the letter of Philippians. Most translations render it *conduct yourselves*, but it is a single Greek word meaning, *live as citizens*. Paul intentionally uses the idea of citizenship to communicate his message about Christian conduct, breaking from his usual metaphor of *walking*. This is a significant shift because citizenship was a prized status in a Roman city like Philippi. Citizens and non-citizens alike valued it highly. Living as a citizen of Rome brought privilege and responsibility. Paul cleverly spins this highly valued status in society by infusing it with greater significance, because all Christians in Philippi were citizens of a heavenly commonwealth even if not all were Roman citizens (3:20). While Philippians knew the honor of Roman citizenship, believers were to live up to their higher status. Just as Philippian citizens represented Rome away from Rome, so Christians are a heavenly colony representing God on earth.

Richard Croft, 2009

Meaning of Key Terms

Key word or phrase	Meaning and significance
A sign… of their destruction, but of salvation for you (1:28)	Paul exhorts the Philippian believers to live as citizens worthy of the gospel. This includes standing against intimidation by those in society who oppose the Christian faith. The amount of opposition from secular culture, whether passive or aggressive can easily frighten believers, pushing them into subtle compromises or even complete silence about their faith. Fearless Christian living attracts the attention of those who oppose the Christian faith and heightens hostility. When Christians live out their heavenly citizenship as Christ has called them to, this demonstrates their coming glorification. When opponents antagonize Christians for their faith, it proves that they are heading for God's judgment. God will vindicate believers who face opposition from the world. In the meantime, Christians will be uncomfortable in a society that rejects God.
If…, if…, if…, if… (2:1)	With four "if" clauses, it may appear as though Paul doubts whether his Philippian readers are actually Christians. Is Paul implying these are not realities in the experience of the Philippian church? Absolutely not. The apostle is using a literary or grammatical device called a *first class conditional clause*. By using an "if" clause, he is actually acknowledging the reality of these emotions. We could even read these sentences as *[since] there is any encouragement in Christ, [since] any comfort from love, [since] any fellowship in the Spirit, [since] any affection and mercy*… The conditions are actual, not doubtful. Paul knows these Philippians are Christians and is declaring four emotional truths to encourage them to complete his joy.

Copy of a replica of Francesco Solimena, 1730

The Love of Roman Gods
The culture of the Roman Empire embraced the beauty and power of the mythological Roman gods. Its opposition to the Christian worship of one God made life very difficult for Philippian Christians.

The Majesty of Rome
The city of Rome with it's advanced architecture impressed observers with the greatness of Rome and made Roman citizenship something to be held in high esteem. The Forum and its surrounding arcade portrayed below are an example of this architecture.

What about the culture?
We have already seen the high social value of Roman citizenship in a city like Philippi. It is important to learn a little more about it in order to understand how Paul uses this concept to instruct believers concerning Christian living.

Roman citizenship granted social standing in a world where status was one of the highest values. There were privileges and responsibilities associated

Giovanni Battista Piranesi, 1756–1778

400	300	200	100	B.C. 1 A.D.	100 A.D.

Roman Republic — 31 | 27 — Roman Empire

Assassination of Julius Caesar 44

Enrique Simonet, 1887

The Beheading of Paul

Eusebius was a Christian historian in the 3rd and 4th century A.D. He wrote of the death of Paul by beheading in Rome under Emperor Nero. In contrast, Peter was said to die by crucifixion because he was not a Roman citizen. Beheading was the quick and dignified means of execution for Roman citizens.

Eusebius Ecclesiastical History 2.25.5

Epistle to Diognetus

The *Epistle to Diognetus* is a second century A.D. Christian writing, which defends the faith and acknowledges the ongoing Christian self-understanding of heavenly citizenship. With reference to Christians, it states:
Their existence is on earth, but their citizenship is in heaven.
(The Epistle to Diognetus 5:9)

The author of this letter is unknown, but a copy of it was found within a 13th century collection of Justin Martyr's writings. Martyr was an influential Christian writer and defender of the faith from the second century A.D.

with it. A Roman citizen enjoyed tax reliefs. Colonies like Philippi enjoyed being treated as Italian land on foreign soil. Citizens were also entitled to military protection, access to leisure events like sports and theater, and special legal rights. For example, Roman citizens had the right to appeal to Rome itself, and to Caesar, as opposed to submitting their case to local authorities. This is exactly what Paul did when he was arrested.[1] Citizens were also immune from degrading forms of punishment like crucifixion. This explains why tradition holds that Paul suffered martyrdom by beheading.

Possessing the great status of citizenship called for responsible and honorable living in order to uphold the reputation of the greatness of Rome. Citizens were also expected to pay their taxes and serve in the military to protect the Empire if needed. It was a great honor to posses such a status.

Paul was not opposed to Roman citizenship. He was a citizen himself, and in the present, he was writing while awaiting a hearing before Caesar because of his citizenship rights. He never implied that possessing citizenship made him feel as if he was disloyal to Judaism or Christianity. Rather, he wanted the Philippian believers, whether Roman citizens or slaves, to understand that they all possessed a greater status in Jesus Christ. As heavenly citizens, they not only had the privilege of fellowship with God but also the responsibility to live worthy of him within a godless Roman society. If Roman citizens were to live worthy of the privileged life they possessed under the rule of Caesar in the Roman Empire, how much more should Christians live worthy of their citizenship with a greater realm and a greater Lord?

What is the explanation?

Let's excavate a little deeper into what this passage means. The first (27a) few words in this passage present the central appeal of the entire letter. Paul calls Christians to a conduct worthy of the gospel of Christ. Paul communicates this concept using the prized Roman status of citizenship. He calls Christians to live as citizens in a specific manner, which expresses the value of possessing heavenly citizenship. Christian living on earth must represent the worthiness of our future hope in heaven as believers of the good news of Jesus Christ.

1. Acts 25:10–12

| B.C. 40 | 30 | 20 | 10 | B.C. 1 A.D. | 10 |

42 Battle of Philippi

30 Soldiers colonize Philippi

27 Caesar Augustus begins rule

Birth of Paul 4–6?

So what kind of lifestyle is Paul calling for? Whether it was the ancient Roman Empire or contemporary life today, how are Christians to live in a way that is worthy of the gospel? The remaining verses in our passage answer this issue in a two-fold way. Paul uses both positive and negative examples in showing us how Christians are to live to express their heavenly citizenship.

b–30) *Worthy Christian living:* These verses mention three things concerning how citizens of heaven are to live the Christian life on earth. Paul expected the Philippian Christians to behave accordingly whether he was among them or not. The expectation is the same today. We do not live out our faith in Christ only if and when a respected Christian is in our company. God is always watching. Our faith in Christ is not something we turn on and off. So how do we live out our heavenly citizenship in a worthy manner?

Philippians 1:27 reveals that the first responsibility of Christian citizens is to "stand firm in one spirit, with one mind, contending side by side for the faith of the gospel." Paul calls Christians to make a united stand for the Christian faith. How Christians stand together makes a statement about Christian truth and the Christian way of life. Paul fuses two familiar images in the Roman world in order to help the Philippians understand the kind of unity for the faith he is calling them to exhibit. The first is "standing firm" which has military connotations. It calls for believers to stand together with the discipline, determination, and oneness of soldiers in battle defending a piece of ground with their lives. They depend upon one another. The other image is "contending side by side" and is an athletic allusion. It calls for a team spirit. Living the Christian life in defense of the faith as heavenly citizens is a team effort. We have the same goal in mind and achieve it best working together. It is no surprise that Paul uses these two images to help Christians understand how to live as heavenly citizens. Serving in the military to defend the Roman cause and enjoying access to sporting arenas were privileges of Roman citizens. Moreover, Paul was currently chained to an elite Roman soldier in the sporting capital of the Empire, Rome itself. Therefore, he uses the privileges of worthy Roman citizens to speak of the privileges of worthy citizens of heaven.

Paul´s second call to those who are citizens of heaven is to be bold in the midst of opposition. Intimidation from society is reason enough for

Public Domain

Senātus Populusque Rōmānus

This Latin phrase meaning, "*The senate and people of Rome*" was first used around 80 B.C. and was eventually carried on a standard by each Roman Legion. Along with the golden eagle or *aquila* on top, it came to represent the Roman Empire and was a point of identity for it's citizens.

Roman Soldiers

Paul regularly uses military language to describe the reality of the Christian life. You can find examples in 1 Corinthians 10:12; 15:1; 2 Corinthians 1:24; and Ephesians 6:11, 13, 14.

Yeowatzup, 2010

20   30   40   50   60   70   A.D.

Jesus is crucified and resurrected 30–33?

Paul encounters Christ on Damascus road 33–34?

Paul's First Missionary Journey 46–47?

Paul's Second Missionary Journey 50–52?

Paul's Caesarea imprisonment 58–60?

Paul's first Roman imprisonment 60–62?

Paul's second Roman imprisonment and death 67?

53

Theodore Gericault, 1817

Intimidated

The word *intimidated* was used in ancient Greek to refer to timid horses that broke loose and ran off because they were easily spooked. The first century A.D. historian Plutarch stated, "But as Flaminius sprung unto his horse, for no apparent reason and mysteriously, the animal was seized with trembling fright, and he was thrown and fell head first to the ground" (Parallel Lives: Fabius Maximus 3). Christians are not to be spooked into dismay and disunity by opponents of the Christian faith.

Christian Character

Nothing is more incongruous in a Christian, and foreign to his character, than to seek ease and rest; and to be engrossed with the present life is foreign to our profession and enlistment. Your master was crucified and do you seek ease? Your master was pierced by nails, and do you live negatively?

Chrysostom, Homily XIII
on Philippians 3:18–21

Christians to make a courageous united stand. Opposition will come. Christians are not to be timid in their faith. They must be bold. Moreover, such a brave spirit grows in those who live constantly aware that God is involved in their everyday affairs. Verse 28 makes it quite clear that God will vindicate his people. Public shame was the pinnacle of insult in an honor-shame society like the Roman world. Even though the Philippian Christians were experiencing social shame and persecution, God would have the last say. He would reverse the situation. Opponents would be shamed in destruction while Christians would be vindicated in salvation.

> ## 1 Corinthians 1:18
> For the message of the cross is foolishness to those who are perishing but to us who are being saved it is the power of God.

Therefore, we boast about you among the churches of God for your perseverance and faith in all the persecutions and afflictions you are enduring. This is evidence of God's righteous judgment that you may be considered worthy of the kingdom of God, for which you are suffering. Since God is just, he will repay with afflictions those who afflict you, and give relief to you who are afflicted, and to us too when the Lord Jesus will be revealed from heaven with his mighty angels in blazing fire dealing out vengeance on those who do not know God and do not obey the gospel of our Lord Jesus.

2 Thessalonians 1:4–8

The third conduct expected of Christians living worthily of their heavenly citizenship is this: live enduring suffering for the sake of Christ. Verses 29 and 30 teach that believing in Christ is not only a gracious gift Christians receive from God but also an enablement to suffer for Christ's sake. This makes us a little uncomfortable since no one naturally seeks out suffering. Yet, God uses suffering as an instrument to change Christians for his own glory.[1] It was certainly the experience of Christ himself. Paul's call to endure suffering sprung from personal experience. The great apostle was not immune from suffering. He wanted the Philippians to see their difficulties as God's gracious gift to them in Christ. Suffering for one's faith is not necessarily a sign of God's discipline. It can be a privilege that brings

1. James 1:2–4; 1 Peter 1:6–7

B.C.	1	A.D.	10	20	30	40	50

5? Birth of Jesus

4–6? Birth of Paul

John the Baptist begins his ministry 28–29?

Jesus begins his ministry 28–30?

Jesus is crucified and resurrected 30–33?

33–34? Paul encounters Christ on Damascus road

46–47? First Missionary Journey by Paul

honor to Jesus Christ. Christ is worth living and suffering for as citizens of heaven.

(2:1–4) Unworthy Christian walking: At the beginning of chapter 2, Paul's focus shifts to explaining how Christians are not to live their lives. Therefore, they contain what seem to be the shortcomings of the Philippian church. The Philippian readers were definitely Christians. This is evident from the four statements Paul made about them:

- They have encouragement in their standing before God in Christ.
- They have the comfort of being unconditionally loved by God.
- They have common participation in the Spirit.
- They have received God's heartfelt compassion.

Paul's concern, however, is that these Christians were treating each other according to the values accepted by the society around them where self-promotion was essential to climb the prized social ladder of status. Christians in Philippi were living unworthily of the gospel due to a mindset of selfish ambition, self-glorying, self-importance, and self-interests. This might have been the way of the Roman world—or of our world, but it is not the way of Christ. Tension among the Philippian Christians was not solely external to their community. It was also self-inflicted. Self was at the center of what they seemed to value. Disunity was present among this Christian church. Paul bases his appeal for Philippian unity on an emotional reminder of their standing before God as Christians. If the Philippian believers lived out their heavenly citizenship without dissension, they would top off an already near full cup of joy for Paul.

Romans 8:17

And if we are children, then we are heirs, that is, heirs of God and co-heirs with Christ, if indeed we suffer with him so we may also be glorified with him.

1 Corinthians 10:24

Let no one seek his own good, but the good of others.

Shield of the Trinity

Notice how Paul presents these believers using the three persons of the Godhead. Christians have encouragement in Christ, comfort in the love of God, the Father, and fellowship in the Holy Spirit. The Godhead as a whole has displayed compassion on them.

Suffering for Christ

In verse 27, we saw military and athletic imagery with the terms *stand firm* and *contending* side by side. In verse 30, the experience of sufferings and difficulties of the Christian life in a hostile society are referred to as *conflict*. This term was used in athletic and military contexts too. Not only was it used for a sporting stadium, it was often used to describe competing in the sport. It was also used of fighting on the battlefield. Paul blends all of these senses at the end of his life when he writes in 2 Timothy 4:7 "I have competed well [or fought the good fight]; I have finished the race; I have kept the faith." Christianity is not a spectator's sport for believers.

Praising Humility

The type of humility Paul calls for is defined in opposition to the self-promoting mindset valued by society and present in the church. Humility is not merely avoiding false modesty or not pursuing selfish ambition to advance your own status. Rather, it is treating others more important than yourself to the point of putting their interests alongside of your own. Praising and advancing the status of a slave would have shocked Philippian Christians, particularly those who were Roman citizens and in possession of Christian slaves. Humility, however, was the antidote to disunity.

50	60	70	80	90	100 A.D.

49? Jerusalem Council

50–52? Second Missionary Journey by Paul

60–62? Paul arrives in Rome under house arrest

64 Fire in Rome

70 Temple is destroyed

79 Pompeii and Herculaneum are destroyed by Vesuvius eruption

John writes Revelation 95–96?

Christian Unity

In 2:1, Paul uses four different conditional clauses to reiterate the one point, which we can express simply as *"Given you are Christians..."* Then in 2:2 Paul presents another four different parallel clauses to reiterate the single point, *"be like-minded."* Paul's joy was complete when Christians got on the same page: Given you are Christians, be like-minded.

What is God saying?

Philippians 1:27–2:4 reminds Christians that God wants them to live a holy life within the hostilities of a worldly culture. They are to represent God in a manner that displays his values before a secular society rather than conforming to its pressures. At least two issues make this difficult. First, there are consequences to not following the pattern of the world. We will suffer. Second, Christians living in a secular culture easily embrace its worldly values if they don't stay on the alert. After all, there was a time when every believer was a citizen of the world and not of heaven. The Philippian church shows us that internal tension and dissension among Christians can be, at least in part, their own doing. When Christians act like secular society, the church ceases to represent God, as he desires. Yet, God's call remains. Christians are to stand together boldly and humbly. Only then will they be living as heavenly ambassadors.

The Scriptures also show the ugliness of God's people fighting and bickering against each other. This appears to be a tendency of God's

Where else is this taught in Scripture?

The book of Acts provides a comparable example of the situations we encounter in this *Field Study*. The early church in Jerusalem displayed both the beauty of self-sacrificing fellowship as well as the greed and the pursuit of self-interests, which we read about in Philippians 2:1–4. In Acts 4:32–35, Luke describes a church united in purpose and self-sacrificial love for one another, representing God in Jerusalem in the midst of ongoing hardship. You can learn more about these outside tensions in the chapters surrounding these verses. Barnabas is introduced in the description of church life as a man who embodied the beauty of selfless and self-sacrificing living. He put others before himself out of love for God. Immediately following is a surprising and contrasting analogy. Ananias and Sapphira also sold land just like Barnabas. They then pretended to bring all of the proceeds of the sale to the church fellowship. They wanted to both keep money for themselves and at the same time get personal recognition before the entire church for their generosity. Clearly their motivations were self-serving. In this case, God intervened with the discipline of death. God takes selfish living very seriously.

Barnabas Caring for the Poor
Throughout the book of Acts, Barnabas models a selfless attitude and becomes known for his encouragement and care for the poor.

Acts 4:36–37

Now Joseph, who was a Levite originally from Cyprus and called Barnabas by the apostles (which means son of encouragement), sold a field belonging to him and brought the money and placed it at the apostles' feet.

Where else does this happen in history?

William Carey was a man of *unqualified commitment to God*. He was a poor shoemaker with no formal training in theology. However, after his conversion at the age of sixteen he devoted himself to study the Scriptures and with time, this led him to become a lay pastor and ultimately develop a *revolutionary* theological idea for his day and culture. He became convinced that foreign mission was the central responsibility of the church. From this moment, his life was changed forever and against opposition from every side, including other ministers and even his wife Dorothy, he committed himself to the task of missions. Together with a group of friends who embraced his ideas, he started the *Baptist Missionary Society*, funded by a group of impoverished churches. In 1793, he arrived to India where he remained until his death in 1821. His missionary zeal and his arduous work in the field set such an example to others that he became the father of the modern missionary movement among evangelicals. During his first fifteen years in India, his accomplishments included translating the entire Bible into Bengali, Sanskrit, and

William Carey

William Carey (1761–1834) was born in Northampton, England. He was a cobbler who poured out the latter part of his life as a missionary and translator in India.

Marathi as well as portions of the Scriptures into other languages and dialects. At the same time, he ran the missionary team, and established schools while also working at different capacities. He did all of this while dealing with the mental illness of his wife Dorothy and the death of one child. When Carey first communicated his ideas to a group of ministers, one of them exhorted him: "Young man, sit down. When God pleases to convert the heathen, He will do it without your aid or mine." However, Carey persisted, choosing instead a highly counter-cultural lifestyle that was truly worthy of the Gospel of Jesus Christ. One of Carey's most famous quotes is "expect great things from God; attempt great things for God."

people. Take, for example, the Israelites wandering in the desert,[1] Moses' siblings Aaron, and Miriam,[2] the fight for supremacy of Jesus' own disciples,[3] and the struggles of the Corinthian church.[4] However, the Bible also shows us the beauty of God's people boldly and selflessly standing strong and living for God. Consider the Israelites entering Jericho under Joshua[5] or the communal lifestyle of the early church.[6] In 1 Thessalonians, Paul echoes a similar call when he exhorts the Thessalonian Christians to live worthy of God.[7]

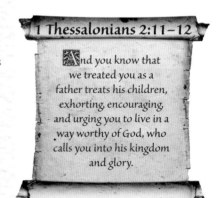

1 Thessalonians 2:11–12

And you know that we treated you as a father treats his children, exhorting, encouraging, and urging you to live in a way worthy of God, who calls you into his kingdom and glory.

1. Numbers 11:1, 4–5; 14:1–4; 16:1–3
2. Numbers 12:1–2
3. Mark 10:35–41
4. 1 Corinthians 1:10–17; 3:1–4, 18
5. Joshua 6:1–27
6. Acts 2:42–47
7. 1 Thessalonians 2:11–12

Prison of Paul and Silas
This is the outside of what has been traditionally thought to be the prison in Philippi where Paul and Silas were thrown. You can read the account of the imprisonment, as well as God's miraculous deliverance in Acts 16:16–40.

Todd Bolen, www.BiblePlaces.com

What does God want?

We are now ready to think through what God wants us to do with what he is saying in this passage of Philippians. Let's examine one main area of application here. Remember, this passage presents the main appeal to Christians in the entire letter. This means that much of what follows in the *Field Studies* to come will help you further understand how to apply this issue.

Live worthy of God's gift of heavenly citizenship

Living a life worthy of God is a profound responsibility. Those privileged with a relationship with God have the duty to live out his values in the world. Christians put God on display in a representative way. It's not easy living in a society that opposes God. It can't be. A world under the dominion of sin and Satan is uncomfortable to those who live for Christ. This earth is a hostile environment for you. You don't get a break from being a Christian when times get tough because times are always tough. The privileges of heavenly citizenship carry a great and ongoing responsibility on earth. How you live your life displays your loyalty to God. As Christians, we are not to mix who we are in Jesus with what society wants us to be. Society works hard to fashion you to its mold. Much of the world or much of the media in the world is set on shaping culture, including sculpting you from head to toe, seeking to capture your mind and your heart. A godless society does not just oppose God but works hard to entice you to value its values so that you will live accordingly. If our Christian identity and status is to override all other places that can define who we are and how we live, then we cannot be passive. You live on enemy soil and remain called to display your God. United, fearless, sacrificial, and selfless humble living is your responsibility before God. So, how are you doing? How are you living the Christian life? Do you live surrendered to God? Is this society comfortable to you? Why or why not? Are there areas of *unworthy* walking in your Christian life? It may not be easy to live in a society that opposes God, but it is a privilege with responsibility.

Giving for Missions

The challenge of living for God in the midst of a secular society is evident in the way the church manages its finances. According to the research of Barret and Johnson in *World Christian Trends*, at the beginning of the 21st Century the church worldwide spends more of the money it receives in embezzlements and other clergy crimes ($16 billion per year) than it does in foreign missions ($15 billion per year). Christians spend more than 94% of their annual income on themselves (more than $14 trillion per year). The average Christian on the other hand, gives less than $0.15 per week to the cause of missions.

(World Christian Trends, Part 20 Finance)

Discoveries

Now that you have completed your third excavation into the rich soil of Philippians, it is time to consider what you have learned. Choose the questions that are most helpful to you or your group.

Connecting with the community

These group questions are designed to help you apply what God wants from you. When applicable, think of these questions not only as an individual but also in terms of your family, your community, your nation, and your church.

1. In Philippians 1:27, Paul expresses his most essential exhortation to the Philippians. He calls them to *live as citizens in a manner worthy of the gospel of Christ*. What does worthy Christian living entail? What does unworthy Christian living look like?

2. Paul uses the concept of *citizenship* because it was highly esteemed in Philippi. How is citizenship in your own country perceived? Is it highly valued? How might believers in your country struggle with cherishing their national citizenship more than their spiritual citizenship?

3. According to 1:29–30, Christians not only have the privilege to believe in Christ but also to suffer for his sake. How do you feel about *suffering as a privilege*? What does suffering for Christ look like in your culture today? Is it similar to Paul's suffering?

4. At the beginning of chapter 2, the apostle uses a series of conditional *if* clauses to exhort the Philippians to live worthy lives. What is the significance of these clauses? How can these four clauses bring encouragement to your church today?

5. Compare Paul's statements involving all three members of the Godhead in Philippians 2:1–2 with his benediction in 2 Corinthians 13:13. Why is it important that all three members of the Trinity are presented or implied?

6. Of the conditions described in Philippians 2:1, which one do you believe is the most counter-cultural in the current culture? Which one is the most difficult for Christians to live out today? Why?

7. Consider the list of negative attitudes and behaviors mentioned in 2:3–4. Which of these represents your biggest struggle? How about for your church? How can you cultivate an attitude that puts others first? What actions can you take?

8. What can you do to improve your Christian walk so that you may better live in a manner worthy of the gospel?

Probing deeper

These research exercises are for your continued study of Philippians in connecting key ideas with other Scripture. They require you to look at other passages beyond the text of Philippians and need to be thought of in terms of yourself, your family, your community, your nation, and your church.

1. Prayerfully meditate on the earthly ministry of our Lord Jesus Christ. Read the following passages: Luke 2:41–52; Matthew 4:1–11; Luke 9:23–26; Mark 7:1–23; John 17; John 19:14–30. How did our Savior live in a manner worthy of heavenly citizenship? What do you admire the most of the behavior of the Savior and why?

2. How did Paul show us an example of godly living in Philippians 1:27–2:4? How did Paul also illustrate godly living in Acts 14:19–28; 16:16–34; 26:1–32?

3. Read the story of Joshua and the battle of Jericho in Joshua 6:1–27. How was God displayed in this battle in the eyes of the Israelites? How about in the eyes of the people of Jericho? What sacrifice did Joshua and the Israelites have to make in order to obey God? What can we learn from this account in regards to living worthy of heavenly citizenship?

4. Consider the Israelites when they wandered in the desert. Read Numbers 11:1–5; 14:1–4; 16:1–3. Why were the people complaining in these passages? How does Paul's message to the Philippians in 1:27–2:4 apply to the wandering Israelites? How does this message apply to your church today?

Bringing the story to life

How are you influenced by your culture? Spend one whole day making a list of how your culture influences or tries to influence you as you go through your daily activities. You will have to pay very close attention to see all of the messages and influences your culture is promoting. Your list might include specific examples from:

- Advice people give you
- Advertisements you see or hear
- The nature of your job
- Various forms of media
- Behaviors of other people that are considered 'acceptable'
- The clothes people wear

Is your culture sending subtle messages of individualism, selfish thinking, and a *me first* attitude?

If the Apostle Paul lived in your culture, what kind of message would he send to your church? Write a fictional modern day response from Paul based on his writing in Philippians 1:27–2:4. The response that you write must contain three parts:

1. A central appeal like Philippians 1:27
2. Worthy Christian Walking like Philippians 1:27–30
3. Unworthy Christian Walking like Philippians 2:1–4

What might he say about living worthy of heavenly citizenship and avoiding the hostile cultural influences in your day? Be sure your response directly addresses the list you made earlier of the way in which your culture tries to influence you.

Memorizing the key

Commit to memory the key phrase for Philippians 1:27–2:4, which is:

> Heavenly citizenship demands worthy living

Part of learning the Bible is remembering what the Bible is about and where to find things. Memorizing the key phrases will help you to better understand and apply the key points of Philippians. Once you have completed the entire study of Philippians, you will be able to recite the main point or purpose of each section of Philippians. These phrases will remind you of the entire argument that Paul is making.

Observation journaling

This section will prepare you for *Field Study 5*. You will read Philippians 2:5–11. We have included three types of exercises: some for before you read, some for while you are reading, and some for after you have completed the reading.

Before you read

Discuss and fill in the chart below with what you already know about Paul's letter to the Philippians. This exercise will help you learn and remember as you encounter new information. You will fill in the new information after you have read the text.

Reading knowledge chart

	What I already know	What I have learned
How do believers live worthy of Christ?		
How do we respond to suffering for Christ?		

While you are reading

On the following page, the biblical text is laid out with a wide margin so you can mark the text with questions, key terms, notes, and structures. The verse markings have been removed so you can read it without distractions and have laid out the text with some spacing to help you see how the lines are related. Review the guidelines on *The art of active learning* section, page xi at the beginning of your *Field Notes* for some suggestions on reading, learning, and marking the text effectively.

Philippians 2:5-11

ou should have this attitude among yourselves which was also in Christ Jesus:

Who, though he existed in the form of God,

did not regard equality with God as something to be grasped,

but emptied himself

by taking the form of a slave,

by being made in the likeness of men,

and by being found in appearance as a man.

He humbled himself

by becoming obedient to the point of death—even death on a cross!

Therefore, God highly exalted him

and gave him the name that is above every name,

so that at the name of Jesus every knee will bow

—in heaven and on earth and under the earth—

and every tongue confess that Jesus Christ is Lord,

to the glory of God the Father.

Notes, Observations & Questions

Summarize the text here

Notes, Observations & Questions

After you have read

1. Go back to your *reading knowledge chart* on page 62 and fill in anything that you have learned while reading this section of Philippians. Compare it with what you already knew to see what the text has revealed so far.

2. Write Philippians 2:5–11 from the previous page or your own Bible into a journal word for word. This practice will help you to remember and understand what you have just read. This week, journal your thoughts as you consider what it means to live worthy of the gospel and its impact relating to your own family, community, nation, and church.

3. Now read Philippians 2:5–11 in your own Bible. Continue to reread it each day until you get to *Field Study 5*. This will reinforce the learning of Scripture and help you to better retain its message.

Pray

As we learn the Word of God, it is essential that we communicate with him through prayer. Commit to praying throughout the week alone or with others, asking God to help you live as a citizen of the kingdom of heaven this week. Write your own prayer or use this as a sample prayer:

Almighty God,

May your great name be exalted among the nations today and always for you are Creator of all people and gracious to all your creation. Thank you that you are a loving God who cares for me so deeply. I know I am privileged to be the recipient of your offer of salvation in Christ. Thank you. Thank you for opening my eyes to the truth of the gospel. Forgive me for taking so lightly my heavenly status. I love you God and yet I do find it hard so many times to live in a manner that reflects your values. It is somewhat frightening to think that I am responsible for representing you in the world. Help me to do so in a way that honors you and brings all glory to you alone. Help me combat living for myself. Help me treat other believers, like those in my church, as the allies that they are. I want to stand strong for you whatever the cost. Have mercy on me Lord and help me become the person you want me to be. I commit myself to living for you because you are worthy. Amen.

Excavate the Site
Philippians 2:5–11
Jesus Christ is our greatest role model

Philippians 2:5–11
Field study 5

How is the text arranged?

In Philippians 1:27–2:4, we learned that Christians are called to live as citizens worthy of the gospel of Christ. Our heavenly identity demands a certain kind of earthly living. But what does this look like? How can we know we are living as the heavenly citizens God desires us to be? Paul continues to answer these questions as he introduces the first of several living examples for Christians to imitate. Let's explore this passage together. Read the biblical text several times. Allow the outline below to direct your reading:

Philippians 2:5–11

Section	Bible Text
Example 1 to Imitate: Jesus Christ	⁵ You should have this attitude among yourselves which was also in Christ Jesus:
Humility to the extent of public humiliation	⁶ Who, though he existed in the form of God, did not regard equality with God as something to be grasped, ⁷ but emptied himself by taking the form of a slave, by being made in the likeness of men, and by being found in appearance as a man. ⁸ He humbled himself by becoming obedient to the point of death—even death on a cross!
Vindication through exaltation before all	⁹ Therefore, God highly exalted him and gave him the name that is above every name, ¹⁰ so that at the name of Jesus every knee will bow —in heaven and on earth and under the earth— ¹¹ and every tongue confess that Jesus Christ is Lord, to the glory of God the Father.

As you can see from the text, the first model Paul presents to help Christians understand how to live as godly citizens is the Lord Jesus Christ himself. What a standard! Note the general outline that emerges. A short verse introduces a poetic section, which is divided into humility and exaltation.

What is this passage saying?

What are some key terms and phrases?

The following table includes a couple of key terms or phrases useful to understanding this passage. They will prepare us for grasping the explanation section that follows. Take some time to understand their meaning and significance.

Christology

This is the area of study within Christian teaching that focuses on the person and work of Jesus Christ. It deals with questions such as:

- Who was Jesus?
- In what sense was Jesus God and man?
- What did Jesus' death accomplish?

Polemical Paul?

Paul is encouraging the Philippian believers to take bold stands for Christ, the supreme *Lord and Savior*. He encourages believers in Rome to do the same:

> *...because if you confess with your mouth that Jesus is Lord and believe in your heart that God raised him from the dead, you will be saved.*
>   Romans 10:9

Paul calls the Roman Christians to be bold in proclaiming Christ as Lord and Savior in the city where lord Caesar lives.

Meaning of Key Terms

Key word or phrase	Meaning and significance
Emptied himself (2:7)	The declaration that Christ "emptied himself" has been cause of much discussion, confusion, and speculation. It has become one of the most debated issues regarding the person of Christ. What did Christ, being God, empty himself of? Was it of his deity? Was it of some of his divine attributes? As interesting as some of these questions are, most of them ignore the answer given in how the phrase is used within the hymn itself. It is important to know that the self-emptying of Christ does not mean that he *exchanged* being God to become man. In becoming man, the Son of God did not cease being God at all. His deity was veiled but not diminished. If God ceased to be God, he never could have actually been God. Self-emptying has to do with Christ humbly embracing the form and status of a human even though he had the rights, privileges, and status of God. This is important. Many ancient false teachings within the Christian church that are present today in some Christian cults, owe their existence to a misunderstanding of phrases such as this concerning Christ.
Jesus Christ is Lord (2:11)	We have seen that in the first century, the Roman emperor was worshiped as a sort of human god. The average person in the Roman empire worshipped many other gods but the Roman Caesar alone, being a human deity, was considered "lord and savior." Paul and the Philippian believers knew this. The believers were experiencing trials in Philippi because they would not acknowledge Caesar as lord even though Philippi was a Roman colony. Remarkably, Paul is flagrantly bold right under Caesar's nose; in Rome, under Roman arrest, and awaiting trial before the Roman Caesar himself, he reminds the Philippians of the truth that all will one day affirm that Jesus Christ alone, not Caesar, is truly *Lord*.

B.C.	1	A.D.	10	20	30	40	50

5? Birth of Jesus

4–6? Birth of Paul

John the Baptist begins his ministry 28–29?

Jesus begins his ministry 28–30?

Jesus is crucified and resurrected 30–33?

33–34? Paul encounters Christ on Damascus road

46–47? First Missionary Journey by Paul

Meaning of Key Terms

Key word or phrase	Meaning and significance
Jesus Christ is Lord *(continued)*	All people will one day affirm this truth, but Paul wanted the Philippians to stand strong with him in affirming it in the present, despite the difficulty this would surely bring.

Hymns in the Early Church

Singing hymns was popular in the early Christian church. We see evidence of this both in and outside of the New Testament. In Colossians 3:16, Paul exhorts the believers to encourage one another "with all wisdom, singing psalms, hymns, and spiritual songs..."

What about the culture?

There are a few cultural issues we must examine in order to understand this passage better. The first concerns the text as an ancient hymn while the second revisits the issue of Christian imitation. We also need to explore the significance of *death by crucifixion* in the Philippian society. Paul's use of this imagery would no doubt have shocked a first century reader.

Ephesians 5:18–19

And do not get drunk with wine, which is debauchery, but be filled by the Spirit, speaking to one another in psalms, hymns, and spiritual songs, singing and making music in your hearts to the Lord,

Does Paul invoke an early Christian hymn in 2:6–11? Researchers, based on the style and language of the text, have suggested that verses 6–11 may have been a hymn sung by early Christians as part of their corporate worship. There appears to be traces of structural rhythm or meter and many other poetic literary devices. In addition, the vocabulary stands out from the surrounding letter as though it was a separate writing that was inserted in. If it is a hymn, Paul introduces it here to encourage the Philippian believers to live in accordance to what they sing in this praise song. Christian hymns have always functioned as expressions of praise as well as ways of teaching Christian truths. They are a form of catechism, so that believers know how to live the Christian life.

Christian Catechism

Catechism is the word used to describe the instruction of the truths of Christianity. According to Luke 1:4, Theophilus had been catechized as had Apollos (Acts 18:25). The teaching often took a question/answer format, as well as the singing of hymns or chanting truths to commit them to memory.

Jesus as a boy in the Temple

Luke 2:42–50 records the story of Jesus at age 12, in the temple courts with the teachers of the law. Jesus listened, asked questions, and gave explanations to the teachers of the law. This is an analogy of what a catechism is.

In the ancient world, learning by example or *imitatio* was an established way of education. Imitating a role model was how people learned their trade or even their way of life. The assumption was that this would improve the student's life in some manner and may even elevate one's social status. Yet, Paul puts a different and important spin on *imitatio*.

William Holman Hunt, 1860

50	60	70	80	90	100 A.D.

49? Jerusalem Council

50–52? Second Missionary Journey by Paul

60–62? Paul arrives in Rome under house arrest

64 Fire in Rome

70 Temple is destroyed

79 Pompeii and Herculaneum are destroyed by Vesuvius eruption

John writes Revelation 95–96?

67

Cicero on Imitatio

In the first century B.C. the Roman writer Cicero wrote about the value of *imitatio*. In his most famous work he states:

Let this, then, be the first of my counsels, that we show the student whom he should imitate, and in such a way that he may copy with most care the chief qualities of his model. Let practice then follow, whereby in his imitation he may represent the exact resemblance of him whom he chose as his pattern… But he who shall proceed right, must first of all be very careful in making his choice, and must use the greatest diligence to attain the chief qualities of him whom he has approved.

(De Oratore 2.22)

Christian imitation called for a downward movement in social status. The imitation of Christ was in service to others. Such a counter-cultural move was an expression of a lifestyle worthy of the gospel.

In a society that praised upward movement and had clear levels of social status, Paul calls all Christians to commit to serve and honor others before themselves. In ancient society, it would be inconceivable for a Roman citizen who owned slaves to consider his slaves' interests above his own. Yet, this is precisely what the apostle calls all Christians to do, including slave-owners. The first role model Paul provides for Christians to imitate is Jesus Christ himself.

In its first section, the hymn ends with an emphasis on the type of death Christ embraced: death on a cross. This type of death was considered an act of public humiliation. It was so shameful that Roman citizens were not to mention or even think of it. Look at what the ancient Roman writer Cicero says concerning the cross:

> "… the very word 'cross' let it be far removed from not only the bodies of Roman citizens but even their thoughts, their eyes, and their ears… the mere mention is unworthy of a Roman citizen and a free man."

(Cicero, Pro Rabirius, 16).

To sing in praise to one who died on a cross would have shocked the Roman society. To declare him "lord" would have added insult to injury. As a result, Romans and Greeks would have viewed the worship of a crucified person as foolish. Jews also considered their Messiah dying by crucifixion to be very insulting.

What is the explanation?

Let's examine in detail what God is saying in Philippians 2:5–11. It is easy to look solely at issues related to the person of Christ, but remember that the point of this passage is practical. Paul's purpose is not merely to teach us about who Christ is. It is to show us Christ's example so that we may imitate him.

Philippians 2:5 functions as both a transition and a summary. It transitions us from

The Crucifixion of Christ

While some artwork presents Christ's crucifixion as noble, it was in fact a humiliating event.

Marco Palmezzano, 1480–1500

30–33? Jesus is crucified and resurrected

67? Death of Paul

155 Martyrdom of Polycarp

the request that believers live as citizens worthy of the gospel of Christ into the first practical illustration that models how this is done. The verse also introduces Jesus Christ, the role model believers are to imitate. If you are to live as God desires you to live, then you must cultivate a certain mindset in life, rather than be conformed to the culture around you. The attitude believers are to nurture within and among themselves is modeled after Jesus Christ, the highest of standards. Only in exhibiting a Christ-like attitude toward one another can the self-centeredness described in verses 3 and 4 be removed.

(5) So what is the mindset Christ models for believers? What is the attitude we are to develop and exhibit toward one another? The

1 Corinthians 1:22–24

For Jews demand miraculous signs and Greeks ask for wisdom, but we preach about a crucified Christ, a stumbling block to Jews and foolishness to Gentiles. But to those who are called, both Jews and Greeks, Christ is the power of God and the wisdom of God.

Philippians 2:3–4

Instead of being motivated by selfish ambition or vain conceit, each of you in humility should consider others more significant than yourselves. Each of you should look out not only for your own interests, but also for the interests of others.

Son of God, Jesus Christ

This early Christian hymn used by Paul in 2:5–11 demonstrates Jesus as an example for Christians. It also teaches much about the person of Jesus. This Christology affirms Jesus as God the Son who became a man. The incarnation of the eternal Son of God was not an exchange of a divine nature for a human nature, nor was it the mixture of the two, but rather the union of two distinct, unmixed natures in the one person.

The Declaration of Chalcedon A.D. 451

THEREFORE, FOLLOWING THE HOLY FATHERS, WE ALL WITH ONE ACCORD TEACH MEN TO ACKNOWLEDGE ONE AND THE SAME SON, OUR LORD JESUS CHRIST, AT ONCE COMPLETE IN GODHEAD AND COMPLETE IN MANHOOD, TRULY GOD AND TRULY MAN, CONSISTING ALSO OF A REASONABLE SOUL AND BODY; OF ONE SUBSTANCE WITH THE FATHER AS REGARDS HIS GODHEAD, AND AT THE SAME TIME OF ONE SUBSTANCE WITH US AS REGARDS HIS MANHOOD; LIKE US IN ALL REGARDS APART FROM SIN... RECOGNIZED IN TWO NATURES, WITHOUT CONFUSION, WITHOUT CHANGE, WITHOUT DIVISION, WITHOUT SEPARATION; THE DISTINCTION OF NATURES BEING IN NO WAY ANNULLED BY THE UNION, BUT RATHER THE CHARACTERISTICS OF EACH NATURE BEING PRESERVED AND COMING TOGETHER TO FORM ONE PERSON AND SUBSISTENCE, NOT AS PARTED OR SEPARATED INTO TWO PERSONS...

The Council of Chalcedon
The church Council of Chalcedon in A.D. 451 expressed this truth of Christ's full deity and full humanity long ago to remove a growing false teaching within the church.

Vasily Surikov, 1876

hymn from verses 6–11 captures the essence of Paul's call to the Philippians. Let's examine it according to its two main parts: humility in verses 6–8 and exaltation in 9–11.

(6–8)

The first part of the hymn highlights the humility of Christ Jesus who, being God, chose to become man. The hymn leaves no doubt that Christ Jesus is God. Before his birth on earth, he "existed in the form of God." The word translated as *form* does not suggest that Christ

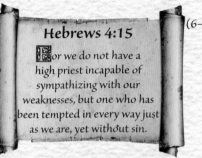

Hebrews 4:15

For we do not have a high priest incapable of sympathizing with our weaknesses, but one who has been tempted in every way just as we are, yet without sin.

merely looked like or resembled God, in the way Adam did when he was created in the image of God.[1] Instead, *form* stresses that his inner essence, substance, or essential nature, is divine. Christ's outward *form* was that of God because inwardly he *was* God. If the choice of the term *form* is not enough to teach Christ's deity, the next phrase in verse 6 settles the matter. By indicating that Christ did not consider his "equality with God as something to be grasped," the hymn implies the deity of Christ since only God is an equal with God.

Christ, however, did not hold on to his status as God. He did not use the rights and privileges of his divine nature for his own advantage. Rather, he "emptied himself." What does this mean? Does it suggest that Christ set aside all or some of his divine attributes? The broader context in which *emptied himself* is used qualifies and defines what this self-imposed emptying is. Christ Jesus emptied himself *by taking on the form of a slave* by looking like other men, and by sharing in human nature. The self-emptying is to be understood in terms of the nature and role Jesus chose to embrace even though he was God. Christ took on a human nature. He looked like a man because he became a man. He also took on the lowly, humble position of a servant-slave. He was one with no honor, no privileges, no rights, and no status. Therefore, the act of self-emptying is simply the fact that God humbled himself in becoming not just a man but also one at the bottom of the human social ladder.

This downward movement in social status is shocking in a world where everyone desired to improve their status. A God

Romans 5:19

For just as through the disobedience of the one man many were made sinners, so also through the obedience of one man many will be made righteous.

Arianism

In the fourth century A.D., Arius from Alexandria taught that Jesus was a created being who is similar to, but not the same as God. This is contrary to the teaching of the Scriptures, including Philippians 2:6. Arius' teaching was condemned as heresy yet continues to plague the church even today. Jehovah's Witnesses are a contemporary group regarded as holding Arian views.

Docetism

Since the first century A.D. some have advocated that Jesus only looked like a human when in fact was not. Docetists believed the physical world was evil and so God could not have taken on a physical form. His physical body and death by crucifixion was all an illusion. Among other reasons for believing this, was a misunderstanding of the phrase in Philippians 2:7, "by looking like other men." They argued that Christ *looked* like men but was not really a man. The context of our passage teaches against this. The phrase that follows, "by sharing in human nature" leaves no doubt that Jesus was fully human. Christ looked like any other man but without sin. Even today there are strains of what is known as the *Christ Myth Theory* which resembles docetism.

---

1. Genesis 1:27

who does not grasp the rights and privileges that belong to his divine status is a God who humbles himself. Moreover, the extent of this self-imposed humility is seen not just in the fact that he chose to submit to death but in the very type of death he obediently embraced. God chose to die as a criminal. Death on a cross to a Jew was a sign of God's rejection and punishment. To a Roman, it was the height of public humiliation. God *humbled himself* to the extreme of a humiliating death.

Raphael, 1509–1510

Disputation of Holy Sacrament
While the subject of this painting is the Lord's supper, Christ is depicted as enthroned above the earth.

9–11) The second part of the hymn highlights the exaltation of Christ Jesus by God the Father. Though mankind rejected the Son of God, he is highly exalted by God the Father. This exaltation is not to be understood as a promotion in heavenly position as if there was something lacking in Christ's status. Jesus is God and God cannot be promoted above his divine perfection. Rather, it is a way of emphasizing the extent and recognition of the exaltation—Christ is super-exalted. How is this so?

Christ Jesus is recognized as having a name that is above every name. It is a name that in the future, every knee will bow to and every tongue will confess. Therefore, the exaltation vindicates a rejected Christ before all creation.

Isaiah 45:22–24

Turn to me so you can be delivered, all you who live in the earth's remote regions! For I am God, and I have no peer. I solemnly make this oath—what I say is true and reliable: 'Surely every knee will bow to me, every tongue will solemnly affirm; they will say about me, "Yes, the Lord is a powerful deliverer."' All who are angry at him will cower before him.

Will all people be saved?

The homage rendered to Christ by all one day does not teach that all will be saved. There will come a time when all will acknowledge, whether they like it or not, that Jesus is God. For believers this will be a day of praise. For those who reject Christ it will be a day of confessing to their shame that they rejected God.

| 20 | 30 | 40 | 50 | 60 | 70 A.D. |

Jesus is crucified and resurrected 30–33?
Paul's First Missionary Journey 46–47?
Paul's first Roman imprisonment 60–62?
Paul encounters Christ on Damascus road 33–34?
Paul's Caesarea imprisonment 58–60?
Paul's Second Missionary Journey 50–52?
Paul's second Roman imprisonment and death 67?

71

God's Glory

The exaltation of Christ before all in no way diminishes the glory of God the Father. It actually increases it. The Godhead being Father, Son, and Spirit do not compete for praise but receive praise as each member of the Trinity is worshipped.

The entire realm of humanity will one day recognize that Jesus Christ holds this *name*. So what name is this? The description in verses 10–11 regarding the bowing of knees and confession of tongues expands on what Isaiah 45:23 ascribes alone to the Lord God, or *Yahweh*. *Lord* is God's personal name in the Old Testament. Jesus Christ will be seen by all and will receive the recognition due to the Lord, that is, Yahweh or God. The reason is that Jesus Christ is Lord-Yahweh-God.

What is God saying?

After digging through Philippians 2:5–11 we are now ready to summarize its meaning and significance. On a general level, the passage adds to our understanding of the story of Scripture. The hymn contained in this text directs our thoughts from eternity past, through history, and into eternity future. It does so by focusing on God rather than ourselves. This broad sweep through history is about God bringing glory to himself. It is about the willingness of the Son of God

Where else is this taught in Scripture?

Romans 8:29

Because those whom he foreknew he also predestined to be conformed to the image of his Son, that his Son would be the firstborn among many brothers and sisters.

It is God's will that believers in Jesus Christ live to become like Jesus Christ. His own public example accompanied by an inner circle of disciples was certainly a form of *imitatio*—learning through living with the master. So too Christian discipleship is about forming Christ-likeness in Jesus' followers. In Romans 8, Paul states that we are called to become like the Son of God, Jesus Christ.

But becoming like our chief role model involves walking the path he walked. Men like the Apostles John and Peter, who were original disciples, reminded their Christian readers that walking in Jesus' path is not only God's expectation for every believer but that it is also a hard trek and it leads to glory (1 John 2:6; 1 Peter 4:12–13). Another Christian hymn that Paul records in 2 Timothy 2:11–13 says it well. *"If we died with him, we will also live*

1 Peter 4:12–13

Dear friends, do not be astonished that a trial by fire is occurring among you, as though something strange were happening to you. But rejoice in the degree that you have shared in the sufferings of Christ, so that when his glory is revealed you may also rejoice and be glad.

with him. If we endure, we will also reign with him." Vindication will come but only by God's aid and in God's time.

Jesus with His Disciples
Jesus' disciples spent about three years following their Rabbi around so that they could be like him and imitate him.

James Jacques Joseph Tissot, 1886–1894

to self-sacrifice and obey in order to bring glory to God the Father. We are reminded in the hymn that God and not man, is the focus of attention. The salvation of man is a means of bringing glory to God; a glory that all will one day acknowledge.

On a more specific level, the passage presents Christ's attitude and behavior as the pattern for Christian living. The hymn is not simply words to sing but an attitude to embrace. It is a mindset that goes against what society exhorts us to believe. Those who trust in Christ are to adopt a Christ-like attitude in being willing to embrace humility before others and leave the rest up to God. Citizens worthy of the gospel of Jesus follow him down man's social ladder of status. Consider Joseph who was a favored son and became a slave in Egypt before rising to rule the land,[1] or Moses moving from prince to shepherd to leader.[2] God's people are to embrace their lowly consideration in the eyes of the world and wait on God for their reward.

Yahweh

In the Old Testament God revealed his personal name to Moses as *I am* in Exodus 3:14. The book of Exodus was originally written in Hebrew where *I am* was rendered. *Yahweh*. English translations of the Scriptures often render this name with the capitalised *LORD*.

Where else does this happen in history?

Athanasius, a short, dark-skinned Egyptian bishop has been called *the Doctor of Orthodoxy*. He participated in the Council of Nicaea, one of the most important epochs in the history of the Christian church. While Athanasius was chief assistant deacon to bishop Alexander of Alexandria, a presbyter from Libya named Arius began to proclaim that if the Father had a Son, then "there was a time when the Son was not." This meant that Christ had a beginning and if he was divine, his divinity was inferior to that of the Father. This doctrine began to spread, but Athanasius and Alexander fought against Arius arguing that his teaching denied the biblical doctrine of the Trinity. The strife was so severe that Emperor Constantine feared the division of the Empire. He sent more than 300 bishops throughout the Empire to a council at Nicaea. The council concluded that Athanasius' view was the biblical position and Arianism had to be rejected, giving thus rise to the Nicene Creed. However, this did not end the dispute, and Arians began a long battle against Athanasius. Athanasius modeled perseverance and long-suffering for the sake of the truth of the gospel. His resilience and zeal for the purity of the gospel caused him to be exiled at least five different times. Four different emperors exiled Athanasius for seventeen out of his forty-five years as a bishop. Among other things, he was falsely accused of murder, illegal taxation, sorcery, and treason. Yet, in spite of the curse implied by his banishment and the dangers, defeats, temptations and hardships he faced, his courage did not fail and orthodoxy was preserved.

Council of Nicaea in A.D. 325
This icon shows Emperor Constantine in the center and some of the bishops from the Council of Nicaea holding the Creed of Nicaea-Constantinople (381).

1. Genesis 37–50
2. Numbers 12:3

What does God want?

Now that we have explored this portion of Scripture, we are ready to think through how we can live out God's will as expressed through the truth we have uncovered. Remember, Paul is now giving you practical "how to" examples of living worthy lives. Here are two main applicational points that emerge from our passage. Think about how real they are in your life now.

Humble yourself before others for the sake of Christ your Lord

Society expects you to want to rise to the top no matter the cost. This is true even if it is through dishonest gain or at someone else's expense. We have our own social ladders that we yearn to keep moving up, rather than down. We dislike public self-promotion and self-praise for it is arrogant, but we want to be promoted and praised and served. Yet our Lord Jesus Christ, the greatest role model on how to live the Christian life, shows us the very opposite. He calls us to reverse rather than embrace society's values at home, at work, and in church. He asks us to look for opportunities to self-sacrifice rather than self-serve. How can we do this? For the sake of following in the footsteps of Jesus Christ, what would a life of humility look like if it were yours? Who can you serve and seek to advance even at your own expense? How can you be a servant-husband, a servant-sister, a servant-employee, or a servant-boss? Is it time to stop thinking about yourself and spare a thought for others? This week, shock those around you by going against the flow. Turn society's values upside down, so that they become the right way up. Imitate Christ.

Allow God to vindicate and promote you in his time

Challenging what society values certainly will not help to advance you socially. You may not get a promotion in work or be recognized for your selfless efforts before others. Expect difficulty to come your way. Jesus did not conform to society's system and was publicly humiliated. His vindication and exaltation came from God but only after his death and resurrection. It is up to God to decide when and how to vindicate and promote you. Remember that as you go about your day today. God alone determines the timing of vindication. Take comfort in the truth that he is just. Appropriate vindication and exaltation will come in the Lord's time, but remember it might not be here and now. Christ is not just your greatest example on how to live life in the world but also a forerunner of your hope to come.

---

1 Peter 5:5–7

In the same way, you who are younger, be subject to the elders. And all of you, clothe yourselves with humility toward one another, because God opposes the proud but gives grace to the humble. And God will exalt you in due time, if you humble yourselves under his mighty hand by casting all your cares on him because he cares for you.

Discoveries

Now that you have completed your forth excavation into the rich soil of Philippians, it is time again to stop digging and carefully examine what we have learned and what difference it can make in our lives. Choose the questions that are most helpful to you or your group.

Connecting with the community

These group questions are designed to help you apply what God wants from you. When applicable, think of these questions not only as an individual but also in terms of your family, your community, your nation, and your church.

1. What is the meaning and significance of the concept of Christian *imitation*? Why is it important in understanding the meaning of this passage and its application to our lives today?

2. Why was so significant to the culture of the New Testament that Christians proclaimed Christ as the *Lord*? Why is this Christian doctrine equally relevant today? What are the contemporary *lords* that compete with Christ in today's society.

3. Look at how Philippians 2:5–11 is outlined on page 65. Jesus models the path from humility to exaltation. What does it mean for us as believers to live in humility and allow God to exalt us?

4. Read Psalm 148:7–14 and Ephesians 1:20–21. What are the common elements between them and Philippians 2:5–11? What does this teach us about God's exaltation and worthiness to be praised?

5. What is your favorite Christian song or hymn? What does it teach about God? What role does music play in your church with regard to teaching the truths of Scripture?

6. In what way can the message of this passage encourage you to persevere faithfully in your Christian walk even in the midst of hardship or persecution?

7. What is the essential quality that believers must learn from Christ in this passage? In what ways can you apply this Christian virtue in your daily life? Compile a list of potential applications of this truth that apply directly to your family, church, and community.

Probing deeper

These research exercises are for your continued study of Philippians in connecting key ideas with other Scripture. They require you to look at other passages beyond the text of Philippians and need to be thought of in terms of yourself, your family, your community, your nation, and your church.

1. Read the account of the crucifixion in Matthew 27:1–61. What strikes you the most about the events of that day? What do you must admire about Jesus' actions? What can you learn from his example that you can imitate in your daily Christian walk?

2. Read Luke 23:26–46 and meditate in the words of Jesus at the cross. What can you learn from Christ's words? What attitudes and actions can you improve in your life because of Jesus' example?

3. The way Paul speaks of the cross in his writings suggests that he also struggled with the common Jewish objection to a crucified Messiah before he came to believe in Jesus Christ. It was inconceivable to him that the Jewish Messiah would die in a manner that expressed God's disapproval. He came to understand the cross to be the grounds for genuine pride not shame. Read Galatians 3:13 and Galatians 6:14. Describe the shift in emphasis that Paul is making. What is the connection between Galatians 6:14 and Philippians 2:5–11?

4. The relationship between humility and exaltation is a common theme in Scripture. Read the following passages:
   - Matthew 23:12
   - James 4:10
   - 1 Peter 5:5–7
   - Psalm 75:7
   - Jeremiah 9:23–24
   - 2 Corinthians 10:18

   What do all these passages teach about God's role and our own role in the relationship between humility and exaltation? How is Christ's example of humility helpful for us today?

Bringing the story to life

Philippians 2:5–11 includes a long poetic section in the form of a hymn. A hymn is a song or poem that speaks of God or to God directly with the lyrics. Two short examples can be found in Revelation 4:8 and 4:11.

Using Paul's Christological hymn as a model, write a hymn of praise to God as a group or by yourself. You can use a popular hymn tune that you already know, and fit your own words into it. Write your hymn as a God-centered poem, based on who he is and what he has done in your life. Keep it focused on him. Make sure your words are rooted in the word of God and that your words have beauty, dignity, reverence, and simplicity. Think of writing words that will benefit believers all over the world, for any generation.

Memorizing the key

Commit to memory the key phrase for Philippians 2:5–11, which is:

> Jesus Christ is our greatest role model

Part of learning the Bible is remembering what the Bible is about and where to find things. Memorizing the key phrases will help you to better understand and apply the key points of each book.

Observation journaling

This section will prepare you for *Field Study 6*. You will read Philippians 2:12–30. We have included three types of exercises: some for before you read, some for while you are reading, and some for after you have completed the reading.

Before you read

Review the key terms from *Field Studies 2* through 5 to insure you remember all of them. This will help you to follow the message that God is communicating through Paul's letter to the Philippian church. The key terms:

- From *Field Study 2* are on page 18–20
- From *Field Study 3* are on page 35–36
- From *Field Study 4* are on page 50–51
- From *Field Study 5* are on page 66–67

Which key terms and definitions have been particularly helpful in understanding the message of Philippians? Why?

While you are reading

On the following pages, the biblical text is laid out with a wide margin so you can mark the text with questions, key terms, notes, and structures. The verse markings have been removed so you can read it without distractions and have laid out the text with some spacing to help you see how the lines are related. Review the guidelines on *The art of active learning* section, page xi at the beginning of your *Field Notes* for some suggestions on reading, learning, and marking the text effectively.

Philippians 2:12–30

Therefore, my dear friends, just as you have always obeyed—not only in my presence but even more in my absence—continue working out your salvation with fear and trembling, for it is God who works in you, both to will and to work for his good pleasure. Do everything without grumbling or arguing, so that you may be blameless and pure, children of God without blemish in a crooked and perverse society, among whom you shine as stars in the world, by holding fast to the word of life, so that on the day of Christ I will have a reason to boast that I did not run in vain nor labor in vain. But even if I am being poured out like a drink offering on the sacrifice and service of your faith, I am glad and rejoice with all of you. Likewise you also should be glad and rejoice with me.

Notes, Observations & Questions

Now I hope in the Lord Jesus to send Timothy to you soon, so that I too may be encouraged by news of you. For I have no one like him who will be genuinely concerned for your welfare. Others look out for their own interests, not those of Jesus Christ. But you know that Timothy has proved himself, that like a son working with his father he has served with me in the gospel. Therefore, I hope to send him just as soon as I know about my situation, though I am confident in the Lord that I myself will come shortly.

But I thought it necessary to send to you Epaphroditus, my brother, co-worker and fellow soldier, who is also your messenger and minister to my need. For he greatly missed all of you and was distressed because you heard that he was sick. For indeed he was ill to the point of death. But God showed mercy to him—and not only to him but also to me—so that I would not have sorrow upon sorrow. Therefore I am all the more eager to send him, so that when you see him again you can rejoice and I be less anxious. So receive him in the Lord with great joy, and honor men like him, since it was because of the work of Christ that he almost died, risking his life so that he could make up for your lack of service to me.

Summarize the text here

After you have read

1. Write out Philippians 2:12–30 from the previous page or your own Bible into a journal word for word. This practice will help you to remember and understand what you have just read. This week, journal your thoughts all that God has done for you in saving you. How has your salvation affected your own family, community, nation, and church?

2. Now read Philippians 2:12–30 in your own Bible. Continue to reread it each day until you get to *Field Study 6*. This will reinforce the learning of Scripture and help you to better retain its message.

Pray

As we learn the Word of God, it is essential that we communicate with him through prayer. Commit to praying throughout the week alone or with others, asking God to help you identify areas in your life where you need to learn more humility. Write your own prayer or use this as a sample prayer:

Almighty God,

We praise you today for what a humble and magnificent God you are. May your precious name be exalted in all the world today for your glorious love for us and your mercies toward us. Thank you Father for condescending to us in your Son Jesus who became like us and died a humiliating death that was ours to die. What a selfless act Lord Jesus Christ to come, walk, and die on earth. Help us Father with the struggle to understand this reverse of priorities in our social endeavors and teach us to act according to Christ's model of servanthood. Our hearts leap with joy because of his holy example to us. Thank you. Help us Father by the power of the Holy Spirit to embrace a life of humility like Christ's life. Help us go against the pressures of society to self-promote and leave our lives open before you. We love you God. We want to live for you in the name of Jesus and in the Spirit's power. Amen.

Philippians 2:12–30

FIELD STUDY 6

How is the text arranged?

In this portion of the letter, the apostle Paul continues to answer the question, what does it mean to live the Christian life in a manner worthy of the gospel of Christ? This is a question that every believer should be able to answer. At the beginning of chapter 2, Christ provides our model. However, some might say that Christ's example is too hard to follow since he is both God and man, so Paul provides two additional examples that show us how to live as worthy Christian citizens. Read the biblical text several times. Take note of the structure of the passage as this will help you grasp the train of thought:

Philippians 2:12–30

Section	Bible Text
Application and Transition (2:12–18)	

General application	¹² Therefore, my dear friends,
	    just as you have always obeyed
	  —not only in my presence but even more in my absence—
	    continue working out your salvation
	       with fear and trembling,
	¹³ for it is God who works in you,
	    both to will and to work for his good pleasure.

Specific application	¹⁴ Do everything without grumbling or arguing,
	   ¹⁵ so that you may be blameless and pure,
	    children of God without blemish
	    in a crooked and perverse society,
	      among whom you shine as stars in the world,
	   ¹⁶ by holding fast to the word of life
	      so that on the day of Christ I will have a reason to boast
	        that I did not run in vain nor labor in vain.

The Work of God

Notice how Paul reintroduces a thought he expressed at the beginning of the letter. In Philippians 1:6 Paul was thanking God because he was confident that God, *"who began a good work in you will perfect it until the day of Christ Jesus."* Now Paul continues to expand on the work of God in Philippians 2:13.

Timothy and His Grandmother Lois

In 2 Timothy 1:5, Paul traces the source of Timothy's sincere faith back to his mother Eunice, and his grandmother Lois. What a blessing to be raised in a godly family.

Rembrandt Harmenszoon van Rijn, 1648

Epaphroditus

Epaphroditus was originally sent by the Philippian church to assist Paul in the work of the gospel. Paul eventually sends Epaphroditus back to Philippi to deliver the letter of Philippians to the church.

Anonymous, 15th century

Philippians 2:12–30

Section	Bible Text
Summary transition	¹⁷ But even if I am being poured out like a drink offering on the sacrifice and service of your faith, I am glad and rejoice with all of you. ¹⁸ Likewise you also should be glad and rejoice with me.

Example 2 to Imitate: Timothy (2:19–24)

Section	Bible Text
Travel plans	¹⁹ Now I hope in the Lord Jesus to send Timothy to you soon, so that I too may be encouraged by news of you.
Christian qualities	²⁰ For I have no one like him who will be genuinely concerned for your welfare. ²¹ Others look out for their own interests, not those of Jesus Christ. ²² But you know that Timothy has proved himself, that like a son working with his father he has served with me in the gospel.
Travel plans	²³ Therefore, I hope to send him just as soon as I know about my situation, ²⁴ though I am confident in the Lord that I myself will come also shortly.

Example 3 to Imitate: Epaphroditus (2:25–30)

Section	Bible Text
Travel plans	²⁵ᵃ But I thought it necessary to send to you Epaphroditus,
Christian qualities	²⁵ᵇ my brother, co-worker and fellow soldier, who is also your messenger and minister to my need. ²⁶ For he greatly missed all of you and was distressed because you heard that he was sick. ²⁷ For indeed he was ill to the point of death. But God showed mercy to him —and not only to him but also to me— so that I would not have sorrow upon sorrow.
Travel plans	²⁸ Therefore I am all the more eager to send him, so that when you see him again you can rejoice and I be less anxious.
Christian qualities	²⁹ So receive him in the Lord with great joy, and honor men like him, ³⁰ since it was because of the work of Christ that he almost died, risking his life so that he could make up for your lack of service to me.

As you can see in the general outline provided, this passage contains three overall movements. Paul applies all that has been said since

A.D. 60?

Chronological Order of Visitations to Philippi in Philippians 2:19–30

(2:20, 28) Paul sends Epaphroditus first, probably to deliver the letter of Philippians

(2:19) Paul then sends Timothy not long after Epaphroditus departs

Why not send Epaphroditus and Timothy together? The most probable explanation is that Paul wants to send Epaphroditus and the letter immediately but very soon will have further news to report concerning his own legal situation in Rome.

Philippians 1:27 when he calls Christians to live worthy of the gospel. In doing so, he is transitioning the readers from the example of Christ to the examples of Timothy and Epaphroditus.

What is this passage saying?

What are some key terms and phrases?

The following table presents a key phrase that you will find useful to aid your understanding of this passage. It builds your knowledge of aspects of this text and prepares you to grasp its deeper significance.

Meaning of Key Terms

Key word or phrase	Meaning and significance
Continue working out your salvation (2:12)	Paul's call to the Philippians to *continue working out your salvation* seems startling at first in light of his conviction that salvation is by grace alone through faith alone apart from works (Romans 4:5; Galatians 2:16; 3:11; Ephesians 2:8–9). Do Christians really have to work out their own salvation? The key lies in understanding the meaning of the term salvation. When Paul calls Christians to *continue working out your salvation* he is referring to **sanctification**. He is addressing people who are already believers and is dealing with the topic of Christian living. In this same verse, Paul states that these Philippian Christians had been living obediently. Therefore, to continue to work out your salvation is simply another way of expressing your Christian faith by living obediently to Christ. Paul is neither confused nor contradicting himself. Works have a role to play in sanctification as an expression of obedience or loyalty to God. However, God sanctifies you through the power of the Spirit, and not the actual works.

Scope of Salvation

Turn to page 19 to review the three aspects of salvation: justification, sanctification, and glorification. Look at the table on page 147 of the toolbox section to help you understand the scope of the term salvation within Paul's writings.

Pantheon of gods

Many of the more famous Greek and Roman gods are pictured in this painting. Religion was a very important part of ancient society and sacrificing to deities was the main expression.

What about the culture?

In verse 17, Paul states that he is poured out like a drink offering on the sacrifice and service of the faith of others. His language evokes an analogy that has two distinct layers.

First, Paul uses imagery from the religious practices of everyday life in the Roman Empire. The Graeco-Roman world of the first century A.D. was saturated with religion. There were temples, priestly orders, local and national gods and goddesses, as well as animals and a whole industry of artifacts to service religious life. The sacrifice was the typical way in which worship

Jacques Réattu, 1793

62? A.D.

If Timothy waits a little longer he can report to the Philippians the most recent news without delaying Epaphroditus (2:23). It also creates some time for the Philippians to respond to the letter so that Timothy can see the effect it had on them.

Chronological Order of Visitations to Philippi in Philippians 2:19–30

(2:19) Timothy returns to Paul and reports on the Philippians

(2:24) Paul intends to visit Philippi soon

83

Christians as atheists

There were so many gods and goddesses in the Graeco-Roman world that to believe in just one was considered to be atheism—a denial of the existence of God or gods. Just before Polycarp, the Christian bishop of Smyrna was publicly martyred in public in the second century A.D., he was asked to recant his Christian faith and so spare his life by saying:

"away with the atheists."

(Martyrdom of Polycarp 9.2)

Christians were deemed to be atheists. How ironic is that today in the Western world?

was expressed to a god. The way it was performed varied depending upon the occasion and purpose. However, it was always a communal endeavor whether it was practiced publicly or within the privacy of family life. Every Philippian was familiar with the imagery of offering sacrifices to the gods.

On the second layer, we cannot ignore the fact that Paul's own mind was so saturated by the Scriptures that the imagery of the life of faith in the Old Testament also influenced how he spoke about the Christian life. In the Old Testament God granted the Israelites a sacrificial system that, through faith, provided the grace of fellowship with him. Different sacrifices were offered with distinct gifts such as animals or grains. Each offering had a specific reason and purpose.[1] By faith, these sacrifices provided a way of living in fellowship with God. Wine was a symbol of joy, and a drink offering of wine being poured out on a sacrifice was a statement of praise and joy in God. Pouring wine on a sacrifice that burned on an altar would cause the flames to flare up emphasizing the offering being made. The faithfulness of the Philippian believers to God was like a pleasing sacrifice offered to him on the altar of life. Paul's partnership with them in God's service

Marcus Aurelius Sacrificing

This bas-relief from the Arch of Marcus Aurelius in Rome depicts the Emperor sacrificing with the Temple of Jupiter in the background.

Matthias Kabel, 2009

Noah's Offering

Sacrifices to God occur throughout the Old Testament, even before God gave the Law through Moses. When Noah left the ark after the flood had subsided, he built an altar and made a sacrificial offering to the Lord (Genesis 8:20–22).

James Jacques Joseph Tissot, 1896–1902

Leviticus 23:12–13

On the day you wave the sheaf, you must offer a one year old male lamb without blemish as a burnt offering to the LORD, with grain offerings of two-tenths of an ephah of flour mixed with oil, as a food offering made to the LORD, a pleasing aroma, and a drink offering of one fourth of a hin of wine.

1. Leviticus 1–7

B.C.	1	A.D.		10			20		30		40		50

5? Birth of Jesus

4–6? Birth of Paul

John the Baptist begins his ministry 28–29?

Jesus begins his ministry 28–30?

Jesus is crucified and resurrected 30–33?

33–34? Paul encounters Christ on Damascus road

46–47? First Missionary Journey by Paul

was like a drink offering poured on top. Together, God received the worship he deserved.

What is the explanation?

Let's dig a little deeper into the meaning of this passage. Paul returns to the call to live worthy of the gospel in light of Christ's example.[2] He then transitions to introduce two additional examples worthy of imitation.

2–16) In light of the mindset of Christ, how are Christians to live worthy of the gospel of Christ? Simply put, Christians live like Christ when they live in humble and sacrificial obedience to God just as Jesus did.[3] A citizen of heaven is marked by obedience. Believers must continually express or translate their standing in Christ into practical living patterned after Christ with an attitude of respect and awe before God. This is to be true whether someone like Paul is present or not. This lifestyle produces unity, boldness, suffering, and humility rather than the self-centeredness Paul had previously addressed.[4] According to verse 13, God alone empowers Christians to live like this. He works in believers so that they can practically work out the life of Christ. God empowers the Christian so that he can be willing to live God's way.[5]

How do Christians specifically live out their citizenship according to the pattern set by Christ? In verses 14–16, Paul gives further definition to living in a manner worthy of the gospel even in a godless society. The apostle states that *obedience includes having an attitude that guards the tongue.*[6] Grumbling and arguing are merely the outward expressions of an inner attitude, reflecting that salvation is not being worked out in awe of God. In adjusting attitudes and tongues, Christians show their character as God's children within a corrupt culture. This removes any reason that society might have to dismiss the Christian faith. They would be like a light shining for God in a dark world. Their very lives would be a proclamation of the gospel. If the Philippians lived in this way, Paul knew he could boast of his ministry among them when he stood before Christ one day.

7–18) Paul summarizes his point in verses 17–18 using priestly language. The apostle expresses his joy once again and calls for the Philippian believers to rejoice with him. Why? The Philippians' participation in the gospel through their Christ-like obedience and their giving to

James Jacques Joseph Tissot, 1886–1894

The Incarnation of God

God became man in the person of the Lord Jesus Christ. This is referred to as the *incarnation* and is the ultimate example of humility. The vast number of artistic depictions of Jesus speak of his significance to people throughout history. God is the perfect model of how God wants us to live.

Sanctification in the church

Verses 12–13 teach about the process of becoming more like Christ so that Christians can live as the heavenly citizens God desires them to be. Believers have a personal responsibility to convert their Christian status into daily Christian living by not resisting God's work in their lives. The process of personally becoming more like Christ has implications for the health of your church. If God is at work in you this should spill out in a certain life among your church fellowship. When Christians grow in Christ, they always look out for the good of other Christians.

2. Philippians 1:27–2:11
3. Philippians 2:8, 12
4. Philippians 1:27–2:4
5. Galatians 5:16, 25–26; Ephesians 2:8–10
6. James 3:1–12

| 50 | 60 | 70 | 80 | 90 | 100 A.D. |

49? Jerusalem Council

60–62? Paul arrives in Rome under house arrest

70 Temple is destroyed

John writes Revelation 95–96?

50–52? Second Missionary Journey by Paul

64 Fire in Rome

79 Pompeii and Herculaneum are destroyed by Vesuvius eruption

85

God's work was a manifestation of their sacrificial offering to God. Paul also viewed his own situation, regardless of the outcome, as a part of the Philippians' sacrifice to God. Together they were expressing devotion and praise. God is worshipped when his people live out their lives in his service in the unity of church community and harmony.

Our passage now returns to provide examples of individuals for Christians to imitate. Paul presents Timothy and Epaphroditus as role models of Christians living worthy of the gospel of Christ. These men patterned their lives after Christ. They stand in contrast to the self-centered tendencies of some Christians in Philippi and in Rome.[1] Just in case Christ is deemed too high a standard, then these two ordinary believers known by the Philippians serve as examples.

The example of Timothy: Timothy was traveling to Philippi to inform (19–2 the church of Paul's most recent situation and bring back a report to Paul regarding their spiritual well-being. Both the Philippians and Paul would find encouragement in Timothy. Paul intended to visit them personally upon release in the near future, but until then, Timothy was a perfect substitute since he lived in a manner worthy of the gospel.

Paul highlights several qualities in Timothy that should be characteristic of the life of those who possess heavenly citizenship:

1. Timothy was genuinely concerned for the welfare of other Christians. Like Paul, Timothy was Christ-like in this regard.
2. Timothy put the concerns of Jesus Christ above his own. This could not be said of those immature believers in Rome who were trying to use Christ's name to advance their own interests.[2]
3. Timothy had a proven record as a servant of the gospel. He had been a faithful servant to Paul for many years and his Christ-like reputation as a servant was well known.

Timothy loved God and people sacrificially. This was very different from the community of churches where few served sacrificially because of competing distractions, personal interests, and even self-centeredness. Timothy truly believed he was a slave of Christ.[3] He loved and served people because he knew and loved God. This is exactly what God desires of his heavenly citizens.

Grumbling in Philippi

The language used in verses 14–18 echoes the experience of Israel. Israel grumbled and argued against Moses and her leadership on numerous occasions while wandering the desert. When this parallel is added to the fact that Paul singled out the church leadership in Philippians 1:1 and made direct appeals to key figures later in 4:2–3, then it is possible to assume that the grumbling and arguing in the Philippian church was in part directed toward the leadership. Bad attitudes and untamed tongues destroy relationships, drain leadership, and discourage church fellowship.

RÉSUMÉ
TIMOTHY
MEANS 'HONORED BY GOD'
CURRENT HOMETOWN: ROME

BACKGROUND
Ethnically Jewish but from mixed marriage
(Jewish mother, Gentile father)
Not circumcised as child because father was Gentile
Originally from Lystra
(modern day, south central Turkey)
Mother Eunice and grandmother Lois are Christians

EDUCATION
Trained in Scriptures from youth
Mentored by Paul

EXPERIENCE: A.D. 50–62 (PRESENT)
Circumcised as adult to minister to Jews
Missionary, servant, messenger, church planter with Paul
throughout Phrygia and Galatia, Philippi, Thessalonica,
Berea, Athens, Corinth, Ephesus, Jerusalem, Caesarea,
and Rome
Persecuted as associate of Paul on many occasions
Mentored by Paul and his most enduring co-worker.

REFERENCES
Dr Luke in Acts 16–28
Apostle Paul in 1 Corinthians 4:17; Philippians 2:19-25;
1 Timothy 1:2, 18; 2 Timothy 1:2; 5, 13; 3:10-17

1. Philippians 1:15–17; 2:3–4
2. Philippians 1:15–17
3. Philippians 1:1

25–30) *The example of Epaphroditus:* Before Timothy had arrived in Philippi, Epaphroditus had returned bringing Paul's letter and alleviating worries for both Paul and the Philippian church regarding his health. Everything we know about Epaphroditus comes from this letter to the Philippians.

Clearly Paul thought highly of Epaphroditus and wanted the Philippian believers to honor him as well. After all, he was one of their own, and a role model of heavenly citizenship that they could imitate. It is often easy to dismiss a local boy, but familiarity should not breed contempt or indifference. Again Paul highlights several of Epaphroditus' godly characteristics to emulate:

1. Epaphroditus was deeply concerned for the well-being of other Christians. The apostle viewed him as a *brother*; a term that speaks of their relationship in Christ and emphasizing a loving family bond. Epaphroditus clearly loved the Philippian Christians with that same brotherly love. In fact, the extent of his distress for them is captured by the word *longing* in verse 26. This term is the exact same word used to describe the agony of Jesus in the garden of Gethsemane.[4]

2. Were it not for God's merciful intervention, Epaphroditus nearly died serving the cause of Christ. He was a coworker and a soldier in ministry who sacrificed his own well-being for God's work. Three times Paul mentions that Epaphroditus suffered nearly unto death for Christ.

3. Epaphroditus also had a proven record as a self-sacrificing servant of God to people. He was the choice representative of the Philippian church to take the financial gift to Paul. He also stayed to minister to Paul since the Roman state did not look after its prisoners under house arrest. Epaphroditus was a practical representative of his local church and a practical minister to Paul. The apostle's needs would have involved anything from caring, cleaning, cooking, and running errands.

RÉSUMÉ
EPAPHRODITUS
MEANS 'CHARMING OR FAVORED OF APHRODITE'

BACKGROUND
Gentile Christian
Hometown of Philippi

EXPERIENCE
Coworker of Paul
Representative delegate of church in Philippi
Representative servant of church in Philippi to Paul
Put life on the line for Jesus Christ

REFERENCES
Apostle Paul in Philippians 2:25–20; 4:18

Wordplay on a Name?

Epaphroditus was a common name believed to be derived from *Aphrodite* the goddess of love and beauty. This goddess is also believed to have been associated with gambling and luck. People would invoke her when gambling by uttering the word *epaphroditos* meaning *favorite of Aphrodite* while rolling the dice. It seems that Paul is playing with the name *Epaphroditus* in highlighting how he *gambled* with his life yet won because it was placed into the hands of the real God.

Epaphroditus' Trip to Philippi
Assuming the letter of Philippians was written in Rome, Epaphroditus most likely would have walked the letter down the *Via Appian* from Rome to Brundisium. He would have taken a boat to Dyrrachium in Macedonia and followed the *Via Egnaita* all the way to Philippi. The journey covered around 800 miles (1300 km) and would have taken several months to complete.

Map: Rome, Via Appia, ITALY, Brundisium, Adriatic Sea, By boat, Dyrrachium, MACEDONIA, Via Egnatia, Thessalonica, Philippi, Aegean Sea, Ionian Sea, 0 25 50 75 100 miles, 0 50 100 150 km

4. Matthew 26:37; Mark 14:33

20   30   40   50   60   70 A.D.

Jesus is crucified and resurrected 30–33?
Paul encounters Christ on Damascus road 33–34?
Paul's First Missionary Journey 46–47?
Paul's Second Missionary Journey 50–52?
Paul's first Roman imprisonment 60–62?
Paul's Caesarea imprisonment 58–60?
Paul's second Roman imprisonment and death 67?

87

An Official Delegate

In Acts 15:2 the church in Antioch chose Paul and Barnabas to officially represent them in Jerusalem. Then in Jerusalem, the officials of the church council would choose delegates to represent them among the churches, and, according to Acts 15:22, Barnabas and Paul were chosen again. Serving as a representative of a church spoke of the individual's esteem. The choice of Epaphroditus as a representative messenger and minister of the Philippians speaks volumes of his reputation among them.

Epaphroditus modeled the exact life that Paul wanted the Philippian believers to exhibit. Here too was a man who loved God and loved people sacrificially. Christian living like that of Epaphroditus implies treating others with the love of a brother, and as coworkers in the work of God. Recognizing the hostility of the spiritual battle, he was willing to serve others even to the point of death rather than compete with them. Like Timothy, Epaphroditus loved and served people because he knew and loved God, which as we saw earlier, is exactly what God desires of heavenly citizens.

What is God saying?

So what is God saying to believers through these words penned centuries ago? God continues to declare in this passage that he wants Christians to live in a certain way even within the secular influence of society. Sustaining this theme in the pages of Philippians signals how important this is to him. God takes sanctification seriously and wants believers to do the same.

Where else is this taught in Scripture?

Moses Smites the Rock

The disobedience of Israel is illustrated in Numbers 20 when the people complained to Moses that they had no water, and Moses publicly disobeyed God by striking the rock with his staff.

Paul's description of living worthy of the gospel reminds us of Israel wandering through the desert. In this age, the church is to parallel certain roles that Israel had in the past, but without following Israel's failed example. God redeemed the Israelites from bondage in Egypt and called them to be his representatives among the nations of the earth (Exodus 19:4–6). The way they lived as a redeemed people, separated from the other cultures in obedience to God's law, was meant to display the beauty of living under God's gracious and loving rule before a watching world. However, the Israelites grumbled and argued their way to the Promised Land, particularly against God's representative leader, Moses.

As God's children, Israel herself had become a crooked and perverse generation according to Deuteronomy 32:5. The nation of Israel failed in being a light to the nations shining brightly by holding out the word of life by the way they lived (Daniel 12:3; Psalm 119:5). Though Israel as a nation repeatedly failed through disobedience, Isaiah spoke of an anticipated chosen servant of the Lord. This servant would succeed where the nation of Israel had failed. Consider the words of the prophet recorded in Isaiah 42. It is no wonder Jesus declared "I am the light of the world" (John 8:12) and his followers are to "shine as lights in the world" (Philippians 2:15).

Isaiah 42:6–7; 49:6

"I, the LORD, have called you in righteousness; I will take hold of your hand. I will keep you and will make you to be covenant mediator for people, and a light to the nations, to open blind eyes, to release prisoners from dungeons, those who live in darkness from prisons..." and be a "...light to the nations, so you can bring my deliverance to the remote regions of the earth."

Where else does this happen in history?

John Wycliffe shed the light of Christ among his generation and became known as *the Morningstar of the Reformation*. At the age of sixteen John enrolled in Oxford University where he remained most of his life. He distinguished himself for his intellectual abilities, and soon his contributions helped to make Oxford the intellectual center of Europe. Wycliffe fervently studied Scripture and came to three significant conclusions that were in direct contradiction to the practices of the Church during the Middle Ages. First, Wycliffe affirmed that the only head of the Church was Christ. Second, he stated that during the Lord's Supper, the bread and wine remained bread and wine and did not turn into the literal flesh of Christ. Finally, he stressed that in order to experience spiritual renewal people had to study and follow

John Wycliffe

Wycliffe was born around 1330 in the region of Yorkshire, England. He lived as a citizen of the kingdom of heaven by continually teaching the Bible and eventually creating the first complete English translation.

the teachings of Christ by reading the Bible. Soon his teachings where declared heretical by the Church. One Pope issued five *bulls* or statements against him. The Catholic Church in England tried him three times, and two Popes summoned him to Rome, but Wycliffe was never imprisoned. He remained under a form of *house arrest* and secluded himself from most aspects of public life. It was during this time when he composed most of his writings and accomplished his greatest legacy to the English world: the first complete translation of the Bible into English. Even in the midst of great opposition by the *Christians* of his day, Wycliffe persevered in faithfully living out the gospel until his death in 1384. In 1415 the Council of Constance condemned John Wycliffe on 260 different counts of heresy. The Council commanded that his writings should be burned and his bones had to be exhumed and cast out of consecrated ground. Finally, in 1428, by order of the Pope, the remains of Wycliffe were dug up, burned, and scattered into the river. He lived a life worthy of the gospel of Christ.

Christians who pattern their lives in accordance with God's will, must live like Christ. Timothy and Epaphroditus were ordinary men who imitated Christ. They served, sacrificed, and suffered for others out of loving obedience to God. However, they are not the only ones who did so in the early church. Many men and women have lived in sacrificial and humble service to God through the power of the Holy Spirit. Timothy, Epaphroditus, Luke, Stephen, Philip, Barnabas, Phoebe, Mark, and many more unknown believers in the early church lived in a manner worthy of the gospel. Believers today can do the same. God is still available to help.[1] Moreover, this passage reaffirms God's desire that those whom he has saved work for him.[2] Christians are still to be a light in a dark world by the way they live because their Savior is *the light of the world*.[3] We are called to live with a love for God and people, while doing everything without grumbling and arguing.[4]

1. Galatians 5:25
2. Ephesians 2:8–10
3. Matthew 5:14; John 1:9; 8:12; 1 John 1:5–7; 2:9–10
4. Mark 12:28–34

Imitating Your Role Model

In the first century A.D., writer Dio Chrysostom stressed the need for intentionality and hard work when striving to be like one's role model. He stated:

For whoever really follows any one surely knows what that person was like, and by imitating his acts and words he tries as best he can to make himself like him. But that is precisely, it seems, what the pupil does — by imitating his teacher and paying heed to him he tries to acquire his art.

Dio Chrysostom
Discoveries: On Homer and Socrates 55.4–5

What does God want?

What does God want us to do with what we've discovered? What demands does he make on our lives by what he has said? Here are some issues that emerge from our study. Remember, there are many more that we will explore further in the *Discoveries* section. Spend time reflecting about how to flesh out these principles in your life. Think through them with the following question in mind: what would my life look like if I was the heavenly citizen God wants me to be?

Express your standing in Christ by living daily like Christ

God wants you to show your relationship with him by the way you represent him. It is every Christian's responsibility to demonstrate Jesus Christ in their daily attitude, talk, and activities. This is only possible, of course, if you are living in dependence upon him. When you submit your day to God, he not only can give you the power to live more and more like Christ, he can also give you the desire to do so. However, when your attitude, thoughts, speech, reactions, ambitions, priorities, plans, and activities are no different from those of society, you blend in rather than stand out. Yet, how you live can be the clearest proclamation of God's offer of salvation to others through faith in Jesus Christ. Can others see, touch, hear, taste, and smell Christ when they are with you? It can be easy to give money and stuff to God and feel like we have done our part, but he wants you to offer him your entire life today.

Self-sacrificial love and service is the pattern of Christ

Timothy and Epaphroditus inspire us to care, love, sacrifice, and serve. They model for us Christian living after the pattern of Jesus Christ. In the grand scheme of biblical characters these men are relatively unknown—certainly Epaphroditus. Yet in this very fact, they model for all of us *unknowns* that we have a part to play in God's redemptive story. Society says that being unknown, unnoticed, and unrecognized is unfair and a failure. God disagrees. Your life is not measured by being spectacular and famous but by your service to God in whatever dark corner of the world you are right now. Who cares if anyone else ever knows? God does. If we Christians were more comfortable with anonymity, self-sacrificial love, and service, we might not compete against one another as we do. How about committing to care, to love, to sacrifice, to serve this week rather than being preoccupied with yourself? When we as a church begin to love like Timothy and Epaphroditus, there is no doubt society will be shocked that someone actually cares.

Discoveries

Now that you have completed your fifth excavation into the rich soil of Philippians, it is time to stop digging and carefully examine what we have learned and what difference it can make in our lives. Choose the questions that are most helpful to you or your group.

Connecting with the community

These group questions are designed to help you better understand the text. When applicable, think of these questions not only as an individual but also in terms of your family, your community, your nation, and your church.

1. Explain the significance of the phrase *continue working out your salvation* used by Paul to encourage and exhort the Philippians. How does this exhortation relate to Philippians 2:1–11?

2. How is the virtue of *humility* related to Paul's desire for the Philippians to live in a manner "worthy of the gospel?" How is our Lord Jesus Christ an example for us in this regard?

3. Consider Paul's message in Philippians 2:14–16. How do these verses offer us an example of Christ-like practical living? What attitudes clearly contradict God's desire for the lives of his children?

4. What is the source of Paul's joy in Philippians 2:17–18? How do you feel about his reason to be joyful? Do you model that same joy?

5. In Philippians 2:19, Paul states his plans but submits their fulfillment to the will of God. This same idea is present in 1 Corinthians 16:7 and James 4:15. How are we to submit our short and long term plans to God's will?

6. Why is it important that Paul offer other examples for us to follow in addition to the example of Jesus in our pursuit of godliness?

Notes, Observations & Questions

7. In verse 21, Paul speaks very highly of Timothy. What were the reasons? Now consider your own local church. Are there "Timothies" in your community? Is your church characterized by self-sacrificing believers or mostly by those who are *looking after their own interests*?

8. What is the most important way in which this passage encourages us to live as citizens of heaven?

Probing deeper

These research exercises are for your continued study of Philippians in connecting key ideas with other Scripture. They require you to look at other passages beyond the text of Philippians and need to be thought of in terms of yourself, your family, your community, your nation, and your church.

1. In what ways are Timothy and Epaphroditus an example of self-sacrificing love? Explore more of Timothy's ministry in the following passages: Acts 16:1–3; 1 Corinthians 4:16–17; 10:10–11; 1 Thessalonians 3:1–7. What other aspects of his character and ministry are worthy to imitate?

2. Read the story of Joseph in Genesis 37:2–36; 50:15–23. How is his response to his mistreatment by his brothers an example for us? How does it reflect the character of Christ?

3. Read Daniel 6:1–28. In what ways is Daniel a worthy example of godly living in the midst of a pagan society? Is there a comparable situation that you might face in your current cultural setting? Would you be willing to stand firm even to the point of death?

4. Read the story on Stephen in Acts 6:1–7:60. Consider the words, attitudes, and actions of Stephen. What do you find worthy of imitating?

5. Words of commendation were common in ancient letters. It was customary of Paul to say a few words of praise for others whom he was sending to a particular church whether that church knew the person or not. Read Romans 16:1–2, 1 Corinthians 16:15–18, 2 Corinthians 8:16–24, Colossians 4:7–9, and 1 Thessalonians 3:2–3. Are there believers that you commend to others as role models like Paul did with Timothy and Epaphroditus?

Bringing the story to life

Like Paul's references to Timothy and Epaphroditus, there are Christians who are good role models for others to imitate. This is helpful in the body of Christ as we can see living examples of how we are to live as heavenly citizens in a world hostile to God.

This week, find a Christian in your church or community who is a good role model for other believers to follow. Like Timothy and Epaphroditus, they should be concerned for the welfare of other Christians, put the concerns of Jesus Christ above his or her own needs, and have a proven record as a servant of the gospel. Describe how this particular person lives in service to others. You may even interview him or her and ask why serving others is so important to them.

Create a short description of the selfless Christian work that this role model does. Write your description is the same way that Paul's does for Timothy in Philippians 2:19–24 or Epaphroditus in Philippians 2:25–30. Share your short description with the person you have chosen. Thank them for being a model of living as a heavenly citizen. Then show this description to others in your church. It may be to your Sunday school class, study group or any other opportunity you might have. Explain why it is important to have godly role models to follow.

Memorizing the key

Commit to memory the key phrase for Philippians 2:12–30, which is:

Serving others is living like Christ

Part of learning the Bible is remembering what the Bible is about and where to find things. Memorizing the key phrases will help you to better understand and apply the key points of each book.

Observation journaling

This section will prepare you for *Field Study 7*. You will read Philippians 3:1–4:1. We have included three types of exercises: some for before you read, some for while you are reading, and some for after you have completed the reading.

Before you read

Review Philippians 2:12–30. Make a list of the characteristics we have seen as modeled in Timothy and Epaphroditus that we are to emulate. Which of these characteristics would also apply to the apostle Paul?

Notes, Observations & Questions

While you are reading

On the following page, the biblical text is laid out with a wide margin so you can mark the text with questions, key terms, notes, and structures. The verse markings have been removed so you can read it without distractions and have laid out the text with some spacing to help you see how the lines are related. Review the guidelines on *The art of active learning* section, page xi at the beginning of your *Field Notes* for some suggestions on reading, learning, and marking the text effectively.

Philippians 3:1–4:1

Finally, my brothers, rejoice in the Lord! To write this again is no trouble for me, and it is a safeguard for you. Beware of those dogs, beware of the evil workers, beware of the mutilators of the flesh! For we are the real circumcision, who worship by the Spirit of God, who glory in Christ Jesus, and who put no confidence in the flesh.

Though I have reason for confidence even in the flesh. If someone thinks he has reasons to put confidence in the flesh, I have more: circumcised on the eighth day, of the people of Israel, of the tribe of Benjamin, a Hebrew of Hebrews; as to the law, a Pharisee, as for zeal, a persecutor of the church; as for the righteousness under the law, blameless. But whatever was to my profit I have come to regard as loss for the sake of Christ. More than that, I consider all things a loss compared to the far greater value of knowing Christ Jesus my Lord, for whom I have suffered the loss of all things— indeed I regard them as dung—that I may gain Christ and be found in him, not having a righteousness of my own that comes from the law, but that which is through faith in Christ Jesus, the righteousness from God that is by faith, that I may know him and the power of his resurrection, to share in his sufferings, and to be like him in his death, and so, somehow, to attain the resurrection from the dead.

Notes, Observations & Questions

Not that I have already attained this, that is, I have not already been perfected, but I press on to lay hold of that for which Christ Jesus laid hold of me. Brothers, I do not consider myself to have attained this. But this one thing I do: Forgetting what is behind and reaching out for what is ahead, I press on toward the goal for the prize of the upward call of God in Christ Jesus.

Therefore, let those of us who are mature think this way. And if you think otherwise, God will reveal that also to you. Only let us live up to what we have already attained. Brothers, join with others in imitating me, and observe those who walk according to the pattern you have in us. For many, about whom I have often told you and now with tears, walk as enemies of the cross of Christ. Their end is destruction, their god is the belly, their glory is in their shame, their mind is on earthly things. But our citizenship is in heaven, and we await a Savior from there, the Lord Jesus Christ, who will transform our humble bodies into the likeness of his glorious body by means of the power by which he is able to subject all things to himself. So then, my brothers whom I long to see, my joy and crown, stand firm in the Lord in this way, my beloved!

Summarize the text here

Notes, Observations & Questions

After you have read

1. Journaling is a good way to help us learn Scripture and is modeled in Deuteronomy 17:18. Write Philippians 3:1–4:1 from the previous pages or your own Bible into a journal word for word. This practice will help you to remember and understand what you have just read. This week, journal your thoughts on how you can self-sacrificially love and serve your own family, community, nation, and church.

2. Now read Philippians 3:1–4:1 in your own Bible. Continue to reread it each day until you get to *Field Study 7*. This will reinforce the learning of Scripture and help you to better retain its message.

Pray

As we learn the Word of God, it is essential that we communicate with him through prayer. Commit to praying throughout the week alone or with others, asking God to help you sacrificially love with a life patterned after Christ's life. Write your own prayer or use this as a sample prayer:

Dear Father God,

You have made it very clear and emphatic that there is a very distinct type of life that you want your followers to exhibit. Even though doing so is not easy in a world of distractions, temptations, and hostilities, you remind me today that others have strived to do so and have done well. Help me live for you in my home and at my work. Help me to serve those in my church. I commit to shining for you in this dark world and I know it begins with things like guarding what I say. I confess my speech is not always pleasing to you or edifying of my brothers and sisters in the Lord. I tend to grumble and complain when I am pressed. I also commit to keeping it in check. Today I desire to walk in your power in the name of Christ Jesus. Amen.

Philippians 3:1–4:1
FIELD STUDY 7

How is the text arranged?

In the previous sections of Philippians, we examined three examples of worthy Christian living beginning with Jesus Christ. In this new section, Paul has a final role model to put forward—himself. Let's explore the example he sets for us. There is great value in reading the biblical text multiple times before continuing with this *Field Study*. This is particularly true of this text given its length and complexity.

Philippians 3:1–4:1

Section	Bible Text
Example 4 to imitate: Paul	

Introduction with a warning against self-righteous Christian living	¹ Finally, my brothers, rejoice in the Lord!
	    To write this again is no trouble for me,
	    and it is a safeguard for you.
	² Beware of those dogs, beware of the evil workers,
	        beware of the mutilators of the flesh!
	    ³ For we are the real circumcision,
	        who worship by the Spirit of God,
	        who glory in Christ Jesus,
	        and who put no confidence in the flesh.

The example of Paul as a self-righteous Jew who became a Christ-centered Christian	⁴ Though I have reason for confidence even in the flesh.
	    If someone thinks he has reasons
	        to put confidence in the flesh, I have more:
	    ⁵ circumcised on the eighth day, of the people of Israel,
	    of the tribe of Benjamin, a Hebrew of Hebrews;
	    as to the law, a Pharisee, ⁶ as for zeal,
	        a persecutor of the church;
	    as for the righteousness under the law, blameless.
	⁷ But whatever was to my profit
	    I have come to regard as loss for the sake of Christ.

Imitating Paul

Paul has already presented himself subtly as an example to imitate. His *gratitude* and prayer for others in Philippians 1:1–11, his *response* within the difficult situation he faced in Philippians 1:12–26, his *team ministry outlook* in Philippians 2:13–18, and his *willingness* to send Timothy and Epaphroditus away though he needed them by his side in 2:19–30, stand as examples of the humble and self-sacrificing mindset Paul desires the Philippian believers to adopt in life and toward one another. In this section, he finally calls Christians directly to imitate him.

Philippians 3:1—4:1

Section	Bible Text
The example of Paul as a self-righteous Jew who became a Christ-centered Christian (continued)	[8] More than that, I consider all things a loss compared to the far greater value of knowing Christ Jesus my Lord, for whom I have suffered the loss of all things— indeed I regard them as dung— that I may gain Christ [9] and be found in him, not having a righteousness of my own that comes from the law, but that which is through faith in Christ Jesus, the righteousness from God that is by faith, [10] that I may know him and the power of his resurrection, to share in his sufferings, and to be like him in his death, [11] and so, somehow, to attain the resurrection from the dead. [12] Not that I have already attained this, that is, I have not already been perfected, but I press on to lay hold of that for which Christ Jesus laid hold of me. [13] Brothers, I do not consider myself to have attained this. But this one thing I do: Forgetting what is behind and reaching out for what is ahead, [14] I press on toward the goal for the prize of the upward call of God in Christ Jesus.
General conclusion and application	[15] Therefore, let those of us who are mature think this way. And if you think otherwise, God will reveal that also to you. [16] Only let us live up to what we have already attained. [17] Brothers, join with others in imitating me, and observe those who walk according to the pattern you have in us. [18] For many, about whom I have often told you and now with tears, walk as enemies of the cross of Christ. [19] Their end is destruction, their god is the belly, their glory is in their shame, their mind is on earthly things. [20] But our citizenship is in heaven, and we await a Savior from there, the Lord Jesus Christ, [21] who will transform our humble bodies into the likeness of his glorious body by means of the power by which he is able to subject all things to himself. [4:1] So then, my brothers whom I long to see, my joy and crown, stand firm in the Lord in this way, my beloved!

Tension with Judaizers

Paul's ministry was plagued with opposition from Judaizing Christians all over the Roman Empire: Corinth, Colossae, Crete, the Galatian churches, Syrian Antioch, and Jerusalem. This legalistic teaching to live according to the Law of Moses had not yet arrived in Philippi, but Paul had learned from experience that it soon would. In light of the recent coming of Jesus Christ, it is understandable that the first generation of Christians struggled with what to do with the Law of Moses and the practices of Israel in the Old Testament. The church had just been born, many Christians were Jews, and the New Testament was being written.

B.C. 40	30	20	10	B.C. 1 A.D.	10
42 Battle of Philippi	30 Soldiers colonize Philippi			Birth of Paul 4–6?	
	27 Caesar Augustus begins rule				

Paul transitions to his final role model by warning against the self-righteous living he once embraced. He came to see his merits as incompatible and incomparable to a life centered in Christ. Paul then concludes his argument by drawing out some applications for worthy Christian living that serve to close out the entire central section of the letter.[1]

What is this passage saying?

What are some key terms and phrases?

Here are a few key phrases that we must study in order to better grasp what is presented in this passage. They will help you understand the details of the text when we turn to the explanation section.

Meaning of Key Terms

Key word or phrase	Meaning and significance
Evil workers, dogs, those who mutilate the flesh (3:2)	In Philippians 1:15–17 we read of Paul's opponents in Rome and saw that they were most likely immature Christians. Now we read of another group in opposition to Paul. They are described in verse 2 as *dogs, evil workers, those who mutilate the flesh*. These Judaizers desired to enforce a legalistic Christianity. The people described in Philippians 3:2 are not the same group of people Paul describes in 1:15–17 though they may have had the same tendencies.
Enemies of the cross (3:18–19)	Paul describes yet another type of opposition by those who are *enemies of the cross*. Are these the same Judaizing Christians mentioned in verse 2? Probably not. The description of these opponents seems to be of those living with no rules or limitations and indulging in a sinful life. The *enemies of the cross* are most likely the people of Philippi who marginalized the believers for embracing Christ rather than conforming to society's values. Living as heavenly citizens draws opposition from society and possibly from other Christians.
Knowing Christ Jesus (1:6)	Paul's primary goal in life was to know Christ fully. He achieved all that his Jewish society offered only to find it meaningless compared to actually knowing Jesus Christ. Remember, as a Pharisee, Paul knew *about* God but never knew God. The knowledge of Christ that Paul speaks of in this passage is not just information about Christ. He speaks of a personal relationship with Jesus characterized by interaction and intimacy between two personal beings. It was not a relationship between a person and a topic. Paul knew Christ in a relational sense, not just an informational sense. His goal was to put all else aside and live in a way that helped him experience Christ to the fullest on a regular basis.

Knowing God?

When Paul encountered Christ on the road to Damascus, his life began to be transformed because he had finally met his Savior. Today there are too many people even in church who know a lot about God but do not actually know him. Are you one?

1. Philippians 1:27–4:1

| 20 | 30 | 40 | 50 | 60 | 70 A.D. |

Jesus is crucified and resurrected 30–33?

Paul encounters Christ on Damascus road 33–34?

Paul's First Missionary Journey 46–47?

Paul's Second Missionary Journey 50–52?

Paul's Caesarea imprisonment 58–60?

Paul's first Roman imprisonment 60–62?

Paul's second Roman imprisonment and death 67?

99

Common Jewish Sects

There were several common Jewish sects or subgroups in New Testament times. Look at the table on page 148 of the toolbox section to help you understand the various common sects of Judaism and what we know about them.

What about the culture?

A few background issues must be highlighted to appreciate what lies behind much of what Paul says in this passage. In the Roman culture of Philippi, a Jewish version of Christianity was tempting to believers for practical reasons. Most of all, it reduced some of the dangers and social persecution faced from the Roman state.

The Jewish religion was ethnically defined. Judaism claimed God and his Law as the rule for life and practice. However, there were many different expressions of Judaism: Sadducees and Herodians who were secular aristocrats, militant political zealots, Bible-thumping Pharisees, and ascetic Essenes. Paul was a Pharisee. This popular sect guarded, interpreted, and enforced God's Law in everyday life and had became very legalistic over time. This explains Jesus' strong words against them[1] as well as Paul's opposition to the Pharisaic mindset within the church.[2]

Rome considered Judaism a legal religion or *religio licita*. This meant that Jews were allowed to practice their faith and were exempt from participating in Roman sacrifices. Moreover, Rome viewed Judaism as a single entity. Therefore, Christianity was an enigma to Rome since it looked like another sect of Judaism despite Judaism's opposition to it. In fact, Paul was under house arrest in Rome while the Roman authorities tried to figure out what to do with Christianity. Christians, who lived like Jews in the eyes of outsiders like the Roman authorities, could avoid many difficulties. Judaizing Christians would eventually come to Philippi and the Philippian believers would be tempted to embrace this false strain of Christianity in order to diffuse some of the tension they were experiencing by not worshipping Caesar and the Roman gods without legal reason. However, difficulty was not to be avoided by sacrificing one's faith in hiding. To know Christ was to share in his sufferings and to be like him in his death.[3]

What is the explanation?

Let us take some time now to examine the example of Paul in this passage. The central section of the letter, in which role models for Christian living are presented, ends with the example of Paul. The word *finally* at the beginning of chapter 3 signals the transition to this final illustration. Paul bursts into an unapologetic call to rejoice in God. Not only because his mind is filled with thoughts of the Christ-like examples of Timothy and Epaphroditus, but also because he knows of the change that God brought about in his own life. Paul

(1–3)

Ananias restoring the sight of Saul
Saul was blinded when he encountered the risen Christ on the road to Damascus. This was the beginning of the lifelong suffering that he would endure for the sake of the gospel.

Pietro De Cortana, 1631

1. Matthew 23:1–39
2. Philippians 3:2
3. Philippians 3:10

| B.C. | 1 | A.D. | | 10 | | 20 | | 30 | | 40 | | 50 |

5? Birth of Jesus

4–6? Birth of Paul

John the Baptist begins his ministry 28–29?

Jesus begins his ministry 28–30?

Jesus is crucified and resurrected 30–33?

33–34? Paul encounters Christ on Damascus road

46–47? First Missionar Journey by Pau

introduces his example with a sober warning. The Philippian believers are to watch out for those who would come to them and entice them to add a Jewish lifestyle as a requirement to their faith in Jesus for salvation. While it might make life a little easier in Philippi, salvation by faith in Jesus is not completed with additional works. Let's examine more closely how Paul makes his emphatic point.

Ephesians 2:8–10

For it is by grace you have been saved, through faith—and this not from yourselves, it is the gift of God—not by works, so that no one can boast. For we are God's workmanship, created in Christ Jesus to do good works, which God prepared in advance for us to do.

Pietro De Cortana, 1631

Gentiles as Dogs

The entrance to ancient Roman homes often had mosaics depicting a dog on a leash with the phrase *Cave Canem* meaning *beware of the dog*. Dwellers of a Roman colony city like Philippi would have been familiar with this type of warning grasping the double sense Paul is making of the phrase when he warns them about the Judaizing dogs. Paul spins a familiar household phrase and applies it ironically of those who tended to view others, not themselves, as dogs.

Three times in verse 2 Paul cries out, *beware… beware… beware!* He clearly warns against negative role models just as he advocates positive ones. Paul turns the tables on these Judaizers. Normally it was Jews who referred to Gentiles as *dogs* but here, Paul uses the word to refer to those advocating a Jewish-flavored Christianity. The ancients did not view dogs as the cute, cuddly pets as many do today. They were dirty and dangerous scavengers. This was an insulting label reserved for those opposed to the one true God.[4] Teachers of this type of legalistic faith sniffed out many of the churches Paul planted in order to mark them as their territory. Paul knew that one day these evildoers would arrive in Philippi. Labeling them *evil workers* is again ironic. Evil workers were those who did not live by God's law in the Old Testament,[5] which is exactly these Judaizers' point. The problem was they were using the law to achieve what it was never designed to achieve and in doing so, they were defying God's will. This was in itself evil. They were also those who *mutilated the flesh*. Their cutting of the male foreskin with self-righteous motivations could not be seen as the circumcision God desired in the Old Testament. As such, it simply amounted to what pagan worshippers did when they cut and mutilated themselves to invoke their false gods.

Prophets of Baal

When Elijah confronted the prophets of Baal on Mount Carmel, the pagan worshipers slashed themselves with swords and spears to try and invoke Baal to send down fire to the altar in 1 Kings 18:28.

In contrast to these legalists, Paul and the Philippian Christians were *the true circumcision*, believers within the Christian church whose *hearts* were circumcised by God. They were living a life of worship, which did not rest on any personal act or merit but by the power of the Holy Spirit. It was a life that boasted only on the merits of Jesus Christ.[6]

4.   1 Samuel 17:43; 24:14; 2 Samuel 9:8; 16:9; 2 Kings 8:13; Proverbs 26:11; Isaiah 56:10–11; Matthew 7:6
5.   Psalm 1:1–6
6.   Deuteronomy 10:16; 30:6; Jeremiah 4:4; 9:25–26; Ezekiel 44:7; Galatians 5:6; 6:15

Gustave Doré, 1866

49? Jerusalem Council

50–52? Second Missionary Journey by Paul

60–62? Paul arrives in Rome under house arrest

64 Fire in Rome

70 Temple is destroyed

79 Pompeii and Herculaneum are destroyed by Vesuvius eruption

John writes Revelation 95–96?

The "Boasting" Game

Paul's résumé of suffering for Christ was remarkable. He reluctantly presents it in 2 Corinthians 11:16–28 in response to other opponents within the church. There are two important things to note. First, Paul expected the Christian life to involve suffering and rejection. We would do well to remember this. Second, Paul plays the *boasting* game his opponents so enjoy. He does so reluctantly in Corinthians and in Philippians 3:4–6 as Paul is not arrogant. It's as though he is forced to talk the language his opponents understand. He can play their game too and show them up.

The warning Paul provides before delving into his own life story is even more powerful when seen in the light of his qualifications to talk about self-righteous living. The apostle was the role model when it came to living life as though one's own good works satisfied God. Paul is simply calling the Philippian Christians to guard themselves against living out their faith with the type of mindset and values *he* used to treasure but rejected in light of the surpassing value of knowing Christ.

If living according to a Jewish tradition was reason to hold one's head (4–6) high before God, Paul's credentials were unbeatable. Was it possible to be a more God-honoring Jew than Paul was by birth and lifestyle? He was *circumcised on the eighth day* of his life. This was the right time according to the law and was an indication of his family's devotion to God.[1] He was ethnically *an Israelite*, which meant that Paul was not just a descendant of Abraham but also a descendant *through* Isaac and Jacob, bearing God's promise to him. He could even trace his Jewish lineage to *Benjamin*, the smallest and rarest tribe that produced Israel's first monarch in King Saul. It was also the tribe that contained the city of Jerusalem itself, and faithfully stood alongside Judah when all other tribes rebelled. Paul even spoke the *Hebrew* language in a time when most of Judea and Galilee spoke the related Aramaic language. Concerning his personal devotion to God and the law, the apostle had also become a leading *Pharisee*; so devoted, that rather than sit in the synagogue, he was entrusted with *persecuting* the church of Christ. His Jewish mindset had persuaded him that Christians were blaspheming God by worshipping Jesus, whose death on a cross proved that God had cursed him. Finally, and as a way of summarizing his defense, Paul lived a *faultless life* in accordance to a Jewish interpretation of the law. Paul had an enviable record in the eyes of Jewish society.

Paul viewed his impressive Jewish resume as worthless (7–14) in comparison to his relationship with Jesus Christ. For this reason, all he once took pride in, was now as *dung* compared to knowing Jesus personally. The term is vulgar and shocking. Note how Paul describes

RÉSUMÉ
SAUL OF TARSUS
HOMETOWN: JERUSALEM

BACKGROUND
Ethnically Jewish with Roman citizenship
Born around A.D. 5 in intellectual hub of Tarsus in modern day, south central Turkey
Zealous Jew of Pharisaic strand: circumcised on 8th day, Benjamite tribal ancestry, Pharisee and son of a Pharisee, blameless before the law

EDUCATION
Early Education in Tarsus
Higher Education: Pharisaic training in Jerusalem under Gamaliel

EMPLOYMENT
Teacher and enforcer of God's Law
Tent-maker by trade

EXPERIENCE
Entrusted by the Jewish Ruling Council in Jerusalem to supervise the stoning of Stephen, a Christian, for blasphemy
Apostle of the Jewish Ruling Council in Jerusalem entrusted with persecuting and removing Christians from Jerusalem and beyond including women and children
Murderer of Christians

REFERENCES
Dr Luke in Acts 7:58; 8:1; 9:1–2; 21:39; 23:6; 26:4

Isaiah 64:6
We all have become like one who is unclean, all our righteous deeds are like filthy garments. We all wither like a leaf; like the wind, our sins carry us away.

1. Genesis 17:9–12; Leviticus 12:3

B.C. 40	30	20	10	B.C. 1 A.D.	10

42 Battle of Philippi

30 Soldiers colonize Philippi

27 Caesar Augustus begins rule

Birth of Paul 4–6?

the experience of *gaining Christ* in verses 9–11. In verse 9, he calls it being *found in him*. This means having a standing before God based exclusively on faith in Christ and not works—*justification*. In verse 10, it involves *sanctification* or living with the aim of personally knowing him more so that Christ's power can transform the believer. In verse 11, it climaxes with the hope of resurrection to perfection in eternal life with Christ, or *glorification*. Paul knew too well that he was not yet perfect—he was still alive in a fallen body—but the inability to become perfect before the resurrection to eternal life was no reason to cease striving toward Christ-likeness. Like a runner focused on the finishing line, Paul ran the race of life unconcerned about past honors or failures, but determined to grow in Christ. Jesus was at the finishing line of life, and running like Christ was Paul's purpose. No wonder Paul burst into an unapologetic call to rejoice in God at the start of this passage. He who had been the role model of Judaism was now a role model of Christian living because of the work of Christ.

(5–4:1) In these final verses, Paul draws out some general applications by contrasting how a Christian should live versus temptations believers face. These words summarize and conclude the entire central section on living a worthy Christian life.[2] Paul is confident that those who are mature in Christ will agree with him that the Christian life of sanctification is one of continual growth even though justification has already declared a believer acceptable before God. He is also confident that God will help those who are struggling to understand the implications of living for Christ.

Paul explicitly calls the Philippians to imitate him in his pursuit of Christ rather than conforming to a pagan and self-indulgent Roman society or hiding behind Judaism. Either of these options were like living as enemies of the cross. In living according to the example of Paul and his collaborators, they would live out their heavenly citizenship on earth with the great hope of the coming resurrection to glory. Paul's emotion and passion cannot be contained as he reiterates in Philippians 4:1 the same call that began the entire section in Philippians 1:27.

RÉSUMÉ
APOSTLE PAUL
CURRENT HOMETOWN: ROME

To know and grow in Christ

REFERENCES
Galatians 2:20; Ephesians 1:3; Philippians 1:21; 3:10

Enemies of the Cross

The society in which the Philippian Christians lived opposed the cross of Christ. It seemed absurd to them that some would consider one who died such a shameful death a deity. Paul describes these enemies as ones whose *end is destruction, their god is their belly, they exult in their shame, and they think about earthly things.* This is the very opposite of living as heavenly citizens.

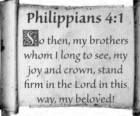

Philippians 4:1
So then, my brothers whom I long to see, my joy and crown, stand firm in the Lord in this way, my beloved!

James Jacques Joseph Tissot, 1886–1894

2. Philippians 1:17–4:1

20   30   40   50   60   70   A.D.

Jesus is crucified and resurrected 30–33?
Paul's First Missionary Journey 46–47?
Paul's first Roman imprisonment 60–62?
Paul encounters Christ on Damascus road 33–34?
Paul's Caesarea imprisonment 58–60?
Paul's Second Missionary Journey 50–52?
Paul's second Roman imprisonment and death 67?

103

What is God saying?

Paul is another saint that all believers should imitate. He descended the ladder of society's status in order to follow Christ. He joyfully embraced a life of difficulty and suffering with humble hope in what God had in store for those who follow him. Paul's encounter with Christ reversed his entire system of values. He no longer wanted to live to gain the approval of man or to have an easy life. His goal was now to know Christ in an increasingly personal way. Interestingly, this was precisely Jesus' prayer for his followers in John 17:3. Jesus spoke of the incomparable value of a relationship with God[1] and warned about living to gain the world at the expense of losing one's soul.[2] God wants you to know him personally and intimately.

John 17:3

This is eternal life: to know you the only true God, and Jesus Christ, whom you sent.

Where else is this taught in Scripture?

God Taking Enoch
Enoch stands out in the Genesis 5 genealogy as the man who *walked with God and then was no more*. He is also commended in Hebrews 11:5 as a man of faith who had pleased God.

One reason God created human beings was to have fellowship with them. God wants mankind to know him and so throughout history he has continually revealed himself in various ways: in creation (Psalm 19:1–4), in the spoken and written word (2 Timothy 3:16; Hebrews 1:1), and ultimately in the person of the Lord Jesus Christ (Hebrews 1:2–3). When Paul calls Christians to live to know Christ, he stands in line with other men of renown whose single desire in life was to know God as well. These individuals from the Bible can be added to our examples in Philippians as role models. Some, like Enoch, are relatively unknown. Little is said of him other than he *walked with God*, which significantly breaks the flow of Genesis 5 to declare loudly, "Man can commune with God!" Others are very well known. Moses, for example, yearned to know God. Like Paul he was a man who had experienced the heights of social status and privilege which the world has to offer and yet, he was called to live a life of difficulty and humility in the knowledge of God (Exodus 33:13; Numbers 12:1–3). King David was anointed to be king over Israel but more than anything he desired to experience God (Psalm 63:1–2). There are also many examples of those who, just like the Judaizing Christians, did not go on to grow in their personal relationship with God. Lot, Samson, and Saul stand out as examples to avoid and warnings to heed. God invites us to know him personally so that we may experience life.

1.   Matthew 13:44–46
2.   Matthew 16:26; Mark 8:34–38

Unfortunately, Christians today constantly find pursuits that compete with their goal of growing in their relationship with God. The source of this struggle is the same source that first century Christians faced. Too often, believers let society's values blend in with those of Christ. Ignorance of what God has actually said in his word, fear of what others might say or do, a desire to fit in, an obsession with our own standards of looking godly before God, and perhaps even basic naiveté about the subtle dangers of daily influences result in Christians who are half-hearted about their faith. We are heavenly citizens who too often, want to live like earthly ones. Through Paul, God wants Christians to remember to live out of love for him instead of self-righteously seeking to earn his love.[3] After all, Christians are to live according to what they are: strangers, foreigners, and exiles on this earth.[4]

Where else does this happen in history?

Mary Slessor was born in Dundee, Scotland, in 1848. Her early life was marked by great need and trouble. Her father was an alcoholic that often would throw her out on the streets when he arrived drunk at night. Mary worked at a local mill factory from an early age and for about a decade, she was the only breadwinner in the house. She was saved at an early age by the testimony of her grandmother. During these early years, the church was the place where Mary would find solace from the family troubles. There, she became very interested in missions work in Africa, where her much admired David Livingstone was. When she was 25, Mary's only brother, who was expected to become the missionary of the family, died. Mary saw this as her opportunity to take his place and go into the Calabar Mission in West Africa in what today is Nigeria. When Mary arrived on the field, it was soon evident that she was special. While other missionaries had found a comfortable and almost opulent lifestyle in Duke Town, Mary was eager to go to the interior and live among the natives embracing their simple lifestyle. With time, Mary became one of the most successful workers in the history of African missions. Her strong character and willingness to procure peace opened the hearts of many to the grace of the gospel even in places where no other missionary had ever survived before. Her efforts lead to the abolition of horrendous practices such as the abandonment of twin babies who were believed to be the result of procreation with a demon. She also stopped the practice of mass murder of the family of a deceased king and many other atrocities. She eventually became the first woman ever appointed as vice consul by the British Empire. To this day, her willingness to live a life of Christ-like, loving sacrifice has made her one of the most well-known missionary women in the history of modern evangelical missions.

Mary Mitchell Slessor

Mary Slessor was a faithful Scottish missionary to Nigeria. She selflessly pursued Jesus Christ above all else for her sixty-six years of life.

3.   Mark 10:17–31; Luke 18:9–14; Galatians 2:15–21
4.   Hebrews 11:13; 1 Peter 2:11

What does God want?

There are many areas of direct relevance to our lives in this wonderful passage of Scripture. Here are some that standout from Paul's example. Take time to reflect upon how these work in your own life. Do not rush reading through them but prayerfully consider their importance. God wants to shape you into his likeness with what he says.

Consider what you value in life

What you value influences your attitudes and behavior. If you value community, you will find opportunities to be around people. If you value integrity, you will endeavor to be honest. If you value coffee, clothes, or cars, you will spend money acquiring them. We are all value-driven people and our values are ranked. There was a time when Paul valued Judaism above all else and this affected how he lived his life. The day he encountered Jesus his values began to change. Your society shapes your values. It tells you what to embrace, what to reject, and in what order. Wealth, pleasure, possessions, entertainment, and self-gratification are primary values in Western society. While much of what you value is not intrinsically bad, God's ranking on your values table makes all the difference. Take time to evaluate what your value system is. What needs to change? What do you consider to be *loss and gain* in life? Why? Where do you find a sense of worth, importance, and acceptance? God wants to change and prioritize your value system to align it to his.

Value the pursuit of Jesus Christ above all else

Throughout his life as a believer, Paul kept pursuing a deeper relationship with Jesus. He forfeited all he once valued in life to walk intimately with Christ. The amount of time you spend on something or someone is a good clue as to how much you value it. What you sacrifice for it is even more telling. Paul descended the social ladder in order to follow Jesus. He gave up his career, his standing, and even the respect of his beloved nation to walk with Christ. If you are unwilling to give him even a few moments of your day, then your value system needs reevaluating. So how much time do you spend in fellowship and prayer with God? Are you willing to sacrifice your time to study his word? Do you consider all other values as incomparable to knowing and growing in him? Your relationship with God will change what you value in life to what is ultimately important. You will end up becoming a better husband, wife, father, friend, daughter, employee, boss, or member of society. You will become a better Christian. Spend time reading, praying, reflecting, and praising your Savior daily. Pursue Christ.

Discoveries

Now that you have completed your sixth excavation into the rich soil of Philippians, it is time to consider what you have learned. Choose the questions that are most helpful to you or your group.

Connecting with the community

These group questions are designed to help you apply what God wants from you. When applicable, think of these questions not only as an individual but also in terms of your family, your community, your nation, and your church.

1. Review Philippians chapter 3. Why does Paul begin the chapter encouraging the Philippians to *rejoice in the Lord*? How does this relate to Philippians chapters 1 and 2?

2. Review the list of credentials of the apostle Paul described in Philippians 3:4–6. What is most impressive about Paul's list and why?

3. Who are the *enemies of the cross* of Christ? What is it that constitutes them as *enemies* of the Lord? Why is this important? Are there enemies of the cross in your community?

4. What is it that made Paul renounce all his previous accomplishments in Philippians 3:7–10? How can you follow Paul's model in considering *all things as loss compared to the far greater value of knowing Christ Jesus your Lord.* How can this be accomplished in your family and church?

5. Why were the Philippians attracted to the form of Christianity proclaimed by the Judaizers? Why was the Judaizers doctrine so dangerous?

6. Christians are called to live as strangers, foreigners, and exiles on this earth. Read Mark 8:34–38, Hebrews 11:13 and 1 Peter 2:11. How are these verses calling you to a different kind of life than you live right now? What changes do you need to make to be obedient to these texts?

7. Just as in the first century, the aim of society today is to climb the ladder of success no matter the cost. What aspects of social pressure are most challenging for you? What can we learn from the example of the apostle Paul in order to avoid giving in to the selfish values of society?

8. Paul warned the Philippians to avoid the legalistic teaching of the Judaizers. Read Acts 21:17–26, 1 Corinthians 7:18–19; 8:8, Colossians 2:11, 16–17 and Titus 1:14. What do these passages teach you about the Judaizers? How has this legalistic thinking influenced the church today? How are we to respond?

9. How are you as a church to help each other pursue godliness? What can you do together to treasure Christ above all other things as the apostle Paul did?

Probing deeper

These research exercises are for your continued study of Philippians in connecting key ideas with other Scripture. They require you to look at other passages beyond the text of Philippians and need to be thought of in terms of yourself, your family, your community, your nation, and your church.

1. Read the following passages: Mark 10:17–31; Luke 18:9–14; Galatians 2:15–21. What do they teach you about proper and improper ways to live as citizens of heaven?

2. Study the prayer that Jesus prayed on behalf of his disciples in John 17:1–26. How does the prayer of Christ communicate the message of Paul in Philippians 3:7–10? What can you learn from Jesus' desire for his disciples that you could apply in your life today?

3. Read Exodus 33:1–34:9. Compare and contrast the attitude, words and affections of Moses in this passage to those of Paul in Philippians 3:4–14. How are they similar for different? How can you cultivate this kind of affection and desire for God in your own life?

4. God wants Christians to live out of love for him instead of self-righteously seeking to earn his love. Read Mark 10:17–31, Luke 18:9–14 and Galatians 2:15–21. What can we learn about how to live from these passages?

Bringing the story to life

In Philippians 3, Paul lists an impressive résumé of worldly accomplishments and privileges, which he considers to be rubbish. His values shifted from his own personal accomplishments to seeing Christ and his accomplishment in salvation as the only thing that mattered.

The way we spend money can tell us a lot about what we value. Write down all the money you spent this past month and what you spent it on. What does the way you handled your resources say about what you think is most important? Did you spend money mostly on yourself or others? Do you give regularly to the Lord's work and others in need? Does your biggest expense show what you value most?

Make a list of your values based on your spending habits and rank which items reflect your priorities. You may ask your spouse or another person who knows you well to help. What did you discover? Are there some things you can change to advance the gospel of Christ in your influence? Remember that every resource we have belongs to God already. Prayerfully consider how you can use your resources to reflect the values of Christian living.

Values:
1.

2.

3.

Memorizing the key

Commit to memory the key phrase for Philippians 3:1–4:1, which is:

> Paul models the pursuit of Christ

Part of learning the Bible is remembering what the Bible is about and where to find things. Memorizing the key phrases will help you to better understand and apply the key points of each book.

Observation journaling

This section will prepare you for *Field Study 8*. You will read Philippians 4:2–23. We have included three types of exercises: some for before you read, some for while you are reading, and some for after you have completed the reading.

Notes, Observations & Questions

Before you read
Review Philippians 3:1–4:1. Write down three things you can learn from Paul's model of living as a heavenly citizen:

1.

2.

3.

While you are reading
Below, the biblical text is laid out with a wide margin so you can mark the text with questions, key terms, notes, and structures. The verse markings have been removed so you can read it without distractions and have laid out the text with some spacing to help you see how the lines are related. Review the guidelines on *The art of active learning* section, page xi at the beginning of your *Field Notes* for some suggestions on reading, learning, and marking the text effectively.

Philippians 4:2–23

I appeal to Euodia and to Syntyche to agree in the Lord. Yes, and I ask you, true companion, to help these women who have struggled together in the gospel ministry along with me and Clement, and my other fellow workers, whose names are in the book of life. Rejoice in the Lord always. Again I say, rejoice! Let your gentleness be seen by all. The Lord is near! Do not be anxious about anything, but in everything by prayer and supplication, with thanksgiving, let your requests be made known to God. And the peace of God that surpasses all understanding will guard your hearts and your minds in Christ Jesus. Finally, brothers, whatever is true, whatever is honorable, whatever is just, whatever is pure, whatever is lovely, whatever is commendable, if something is excellent or praiseworthy, think about these things. And what you learned and received and heard and saw in me, do these things. And the God of peace will be with you.

I have great joy in the Lord that now at last you have renewed your concern for me; indeed, you were concerned before but lacked opportunity. I am not saying this because I am in need, for I have learned to be content whatever the circumstances. I have known times of need and times of abundance. I have learned the secret of being content in every situation, whether satisfied or hungry, whether in plenty or in want. I can do all things through him who strengthens me. Nevertheless, it was kind of you to share in my trouble. And you Philippians know, in the beginning of my gospel ministry, when I left Macedonia, no church shared with me in this matter of giving and receiving except you alone. Even when I was in Thessalonica, you sent me a gift more than once for my needs. Not that I seek a gift, rather I seek what may be credited to your account. For I have received everything and even more. I have all I need for I received from Epaphroditus what you sent—a fragrant offering, an acceptable sacrifice, pleasing to God. And my God will supply your every need according to his glorious riches in Christ Jesus. To our God and Father be glory for ever and ever. Amen.

Greet every saint in Christ Jesus. The brothers with me send greetings. All the saints greet you, especially those of Caesar's household. The grace of the Lord Jesus Christ be with your spirit.

Summarize the text here

Notes, Observations & Questions

After you have read

1. Journaling Scripture is another way to help us learn and is modeled in Deuteronomy 17:18. You will remember more if you respond to what you have read by writing. Therefore, write Philippians 4:2–23 from the previous page or from your own Bible into a journal word for word.

2. This week, journal your thoughts each day about what you value in life and what needs to be done to treasure Christ above all. Consider how your values are impacted by your own family, community, nation, and church.

3. Now read Philippians 4:2–23 in your own Bible. Continue to reread it each day until you get to *Field Study 8*. This will reinforce the learning of Scripture and help you to better retain its message.

Pray

As we learn the Word of God, it is essential that we communicate with him through prayer. Commit to praying throughout the week alone or with others, asking God to help you identify areas in your life where you are not valuing Christ above all. Also, ask him to forgive you for doing so. Write your own prayer or use this as a sample prayer:

The Lord's Prayer

"Pray like this:
Our Father in heaven, hallowed be your name.
Your kingdom come. Your will be done on earth as it is in heaven.
Give us today our daily bread.
And forgive us our debts as we also forgive our debtors.
And do not lead us into temptation but deliver us from the evil one."

Matthew 6:9–13

Dependence on Christ brings unity and contentment

Philippians 4:2–23

FIELD STUDY 8

How is the text arranged?

We now reach the final *Field Study* in our excavation of the text of Philippians. Paul's argument continues rapidly to the end of the letter. Make sure you carefully read the biblical text several times and see if you can identify the divisions in Paul's structure:

Philippians 4:2–23

Section	Bible Text
The Philippian Situation (4:2–9)	
Application for life within the church	² I appeal to Euodia and to Syntyche to agree in the Lord. ³ Yes, and I ask you, true companion, to help these women who have struggled together in the gospel ministry along with me and Clement, and my other fellow workers, whose names are in the book of life.
Application for life within a godless society	⁴ Rejoice in the Lord always. Again I say, rejoice! ⁵ Let your gentleness be seen by all. The Lord is near! ⁶ Do not be anxious about anything, but in everything by prayer and supplication, with thanksgiving, let your requests be made known to God. ⁷ And the peace of God that surpasses all understanding will guard your hearts and your minds in Christ Jesus. ⁸ Finally, brothers, whatever is true, whatever is honorable, whatever is just, whatever is pure, whatever is lovely, whatever is commendable, if something is excellent or praiseworthy, think about these things. ⁹ And what you learned and received and heard and saw in me, do these things. And the God of peace will be with you.

Philippians 4:2—23

Section	Bible Text
Expression of Thanksgiving (4:10–20)	
Thank you for the money gift	[10] I have great joy in the Lord that now at last you have renewed your concern for me; indeed, you were concerned before but lacked opportunity.

Contentment in God	[11] I am not saying this because I am in need,
	     for I have learned to be content
	          whatever the circumstances.
	[12] I have known times of need and times of abundance.
	I have learned the secret of being content in every situation,
	     whether satisfied or hungry, whether in plenty or in want.
	[13] I can do all things through him who strengthens me.
	     [14] Nevertheless, it was kind of you to share in my trouble.

Philippian history of giving	[15] And you Philippians know,
	     in the beginning of my gospel ministry,
	     when I left Macedonia,
	     no church shared with me
	     in this matter of giving and receiving except you alone.
	[16] Even when I was in Thessalonica,
	     you sent me a gift more than once for my needs.

Giving as a product of God's work which he rewards to his glory	[17] Not that I seek a gift,
	     rather I seek what may be credited to your account.
	[18] For I have received everything and even more.
	     I have all I need
	          for I received from Epaphroditus what you sent—
	     a fragrant offering, an acceptable sacrifice, pleasing to God.
	[19] And my God will supply your every need
	     according to his glorious riches in Christ Jesus.
	[20] To our God and Father be glory for ever and ever. Amen.

Closing Words (4:21–23)	

Salutation	[21] Greet every saint in Christ Jesus.
	     The brothers with me send greetings.
	[22] All the saints greet you,
	     especially those of Caesar's household.
	[23] The grace of the Lord Jesus Christ be with your spirit.

Notice how Paul closes his letter by providing words of application for the Philippian believers. Both as a church fellowship and as individuals, they are instructed regarding living christianly in a hostile society. He then thanks them for the monetary gift they sent him recently. His gratitude also provides an opportunity for him to talk about contentment in life. Finally, he ends with a customary greeting.

What is this passage saying?
What are some key terms and phrases?

The table below presents some key words and phrases that will help in understanding this passage. Alongside the cultural issues that follow, these key terms are essential to grasping the significance of Paul's message. Take some time to study and understand them.

Meaning of Key Terms

Key word or phrase	Meaning and significance
Rejoice (4:4, 10)	We have already learned that joy is a Christian fruit found in those whose focus and hope is not on their situation but on God. The joy Paul displayed despite the hardships of his house arrest is the joy he calls for in the lives of all Christians even in the buffeting of life. The strains and stresses of our lives compete with God and affect our attitude. However, they cannot rob us of joy unless we ignore God's presence when we find ourselves in the middle of difficulty. As Christians, we are called to place our hope in life exclusively and repeatedly in God alone.
The Book of Life (4:3)	Paul mentions a *Book of Life* in which names are written. What book is this? Several *books* are mentioned in the Bible. For example, there is the *Book of Wars* with songs of celebration of God's acts on behalf of his people in Numbers 21:14–15. There is also the *Books of Works*, which records the deeds of unbelievers in Revelation 20:13. In addition, there is a *Book of the Living*, which Moses refers to in Exodus 32:32–33 and David cites in Psalm 69:28. This contained a list of people who were currently living. One would be blotted out upon death. These books are not the same as the book Paul refers to in verse 3. In a city like Philippi, where citizenship was granted by birth, it was important to keep a register of names. Since Paul develops the topic of heavenly citizenship in this letter, he uses this very familiar practice to speak of a heavenly register in which the names of believers are written. Paul uses the *Book of Life* here to refer to those who are Christians.
True, noble, right, pure, lovely, admirable, praise-worthy (4:8)	Virtues were praised even in societies not influenced by Christianity. The Greeks and the Romans had something like moral handbooks. The virtues Paul listed would have been recognized in a pagan society like Philippi, and they were therefore not distinctively Christian. Paul seeks here to redeem these virtues back to their real source in God. As Paul calls Christians to learn to evaluate culture through a Christian worldview, he recognizes that not everything in society is bad. Culture can exhibit traces of virtues, which Christianity ought to exhibit without dilution.

William Andrews, 1900

English Doomsday Books

In A.D. 1085, William I of England commissioned a survey of England to record what each landowner had in property and livestock. The survey was used to determine the amount of tax owed and whatever the book said, was final. It became known as the *Doomsday Book*.

Professor J.J.N. Palmer and George Slater, 1066

Page from Doomsday Book

Here is an image from the eleventh century *Doomsday Book* that shows how the records were carefully kept. It functioned like the *Book of the Living* which tracked all those who were living.

What about the culture?

The first century Roman world enjoyed peace. After centuries of war, the Roman state was able to patrol its huge borders and respond to any skirmishes due to the vast network of roads the Romans had built. Roman peace or *Pax Romana* was ironically imposed by fear of the sword. Roman garrisons were located throughout the Empire and particularly in Roman colony cities like Philippi to protect its interests. Peace propaganda on coins and public inscriptions was a way of discouraging opposition now that Rome ruled. However, peace imposed by force does not last. A violent response to violence settles the matter only temporarily. Only a changed heart is able to desire and produce lasting peace, and only God is able to change a heart. When Paul speaks of the *peace of God* and the *God of peace* in Philippians 4:7 and 9 he is well aware of the Roman form of peace. The Philippian believers would have noted the contrast. Ultimately, *Pax Romana* is no match for God's peace or *Pax Dei*.

> **Colossians 3:15**
>
> Let the peace of Christ reign in your hearts, since indeed you were called in one body to peace; and be thankful.

What is the explanation?

Let us now examine in detail the contents and significance of these verses.

The Philippian Situation: Living as worthy heavenly citizens involves (1–2) imitating the role models Paul previously mentioned. If these believers had embraced everything that had been said since Philippians 1:27 their behavior would have solved the problems within the Philippian church, and any other church throughout history. If Christians stand united, boldly enduring difficulty,[1] and humbly imitating the servant self-sacrificing attitude of Christ, Timothy, Epaphroditus, and Paul,[2] then our self-inflicted tensions within the community of the church would go away. We would live as worthy heavenly citizens.

Verses 2–9 are more than the application of the central thrust of the letter. They address

Romans Negotiating for Peace

After an initial embarrassing defeat of two Roman legions, a massive Roman army defeated the Batavi rebellion in A.D. 70 and forced humiliating terms of peace on the tribal people.

Jacob Jordaens the elder, 1661–1662

CNG, 2010

Pax Augusti

Roman peace was established by Caesar Augustus around 27 B.C. and so it is sometimes called Augustus' peace or *Pax Augusti*.

Paul	Philippian Christians
Situation: • Imprisoned by Caesar of society 1:13 (external) • Christians troubling Paul 1:17 (internal)	Situation: • Christians troubling each other 4:2 (internal) • Marginalized by Caesar's society 4:4–7 (external)
Response: • Joy 1:18 • Gentle attitude to troublers 1:18 • Confidence of deliverance from prison by God through prayers 1:19	Desired Response: • Joy 4:4 • Gentleness 4:5 • Confidence of deliverance from worries by God through prayers 4:5–7
Result: • The gospel advancing across Roman society 1:12–18	Potential Result: • Influence society by living out the gospel they received 4:8–9

1. Philippians 1:27–2:4
2. Philippians 2:5–4:1

B.C.	1	A.D.	10	20	30	40	50

5? Birth of Jesus

4–6? Birth of Paul

John the Baptist begins his ministry 28–29?

Jesus begins his ministry 28–30?

Jesus is crucified and resurrected 30–33?

33–34? Paul encounters Christ on Damascus road

46–47? First Missionary Journey by Paul

the Philippian situation of turmoil and strain in light of Philippians 1:12–26 where Paul described his attitude within his own difficult situation. The apostle was modeling a response amidst the strains and stresses of his own life from the beginning. The Philippian church was struggling with both internal and external pressures.

(3–5) One specific internal problem causing disunity in the fellowship was the disagreement between Euodia and Syntyche, two Christians in Philippi. Their conflict had reached the ears of Paul, and they were setting the wrong example. Paul does not elaborate on the specifics of their disagreement nor does he take sides. He simply offers a short solution to this internal problem: come to an agreement for the sake of the Lord. This is all that needs to be said because Paul has been discussing Christian living throughout the letter. He asks an unnamed companion in Philippi to help these women settle their differences. Paul knew that a mediator would help move the problem toward reconciliation with maturity and fairness. These women, after all, were more mature in the faith than what their current behavior was showing. They also had a history of serving sacrificially in the progress of the gospel together with Paul, a man named Clement, and other coworkers. All believers, and particularly leading voices within churches or Christian ministry, must always work to resolve their disagreements precisely because they are Christians. Their names are written in the *Book of Life*.

We must also remember that external tensions also threatened the Philippian Christians. How could Christians live in a godless place without giving in to its demands but rather influencing it through their testimony? In verses 4–7, Paul provides three main commands as an antidote to crumbling under society's influence; then in verses 8–9 he provides sound advice on how to live out the Christian faith.

First, Christians are called to rejoice always. This is an attitude that Paul keeps revisiting and repeats it here for the sake of emphasis. An attitude of joy in the Christian life despite the situation is not a choice but a necessity. Contentment in every situation—both difficulties and delights—is possible only when believers focus on Christ as the source of life. Paul was calling the Philippians to find their joy in the Lord Jesus Christ and not succumb to the pressures of the godless society ruled by *lord Caesar*.

The second aspect of the antidote against yielding to the pressures of a godless society was to be *gentle* to all. It is hard to pin down precisely the meaning of the term translated as *gentle*. Perhaps the following

Euodia and Syntyche

Very little is known of these ladies other than their disagreement was damaging the unity of the believers in Philippi. Their names indicate they came from pagan Greek families. *Euodia* means *success* and *Syntyche* means *luck*. Paul does not name them to shame them. Those he wanted to shame would usually be left nameless so that posterity would not remember them. Consider: Romans 16:17; 1 Corinthians 4:18; 5:1; Philippians 1:15–17.

The True Companion?

Paul does not identify the *true companion* in verse 3. In the second century A.D., Clement of Alexandria caused substantial interest in the issue by stating this person was Paul's wife (Stromata 3.53). Other options proposed are:
- An individual whose name was *Syzygos*, which is the Greek term for *companion*
- Epaphroditus himself as bearer of the letter being read out in public
- Luke, who was a trusted companion of Paul's who ministered in Philippi
- Lydia because the church might have been still meeting in her house

We do not know who this individual was, but the Philippian church clearly did.

| 50 | 60 | 70 | 80 | 90 | 100 A.D. |

49? Jerusalem Council

50–52? Second Missionary Journey by Paul

60–62? Paul arrives in Rome under house arrest

64 Fire in Rome

70 Temple is destroyed

79 Pompeii and Herculaneum are destroyed by Vesuvius eruption

John writes Revelation 95–96?

117

Proverbs 15:1

A gentle answer deflects anger; but a harsh word stirs up anger.

The Lord is Near

This comforting exclamation is general enough to be interpreted in several ways. It can mean that the Lord is about to return (time) or that he is close by (space). Moreover, it could be attached to the command to gentleness (4:5), to the command not to be anxious (4:6), or perhaps do double duty with both. The nearness of God is good reason to rejoice, be gentle, and fill our prayers with grateful dependence. No wonder Christians can have such peace in a world filled with sorrow, unkindness, violence, ingratitude and independence.

Prayer, Petition, Requests

These different words are used to emphasize a single activity: talking to God. Christians have the privilege of taking every situation to God. God allows us to make requests to him through words. What a privilege. However, not that you are to ask of God and not demand of him. This is to be done with an attitude of thanksgiving.

synonyms will help you appreciate its meaning. God wants Christians to be gentle, kind, reasonable, compassionate, patient, long-suffering, tolerant, or fair to those in society who are hostile toward them. Believers are to display this mindset regardless of society's attacks.

Finally, Christians were to be free from worry. How? Believers could (6–7) be relieved from anxiety from anything because God was instantly accessible and available to them for everything they needed. The Philippian Christians were suffering at the hands of a defying *lord Caesar*, but the Lord Jesus Christ was near. God was available. God wants to be called into any and every situation of life through prayer, so that his presence and power can eradicate the burdens we face. More than a cry of desperation, prayer can be a confident call. When we pray with an attitude of gratitude, we acknowledge both our dependence upon God and our lack of entitlement to him other than by his grace. In return, God promises to grant such a depth of peace, that only experiencing it can testify to it—reason cannot understand it. This peace could do much more than the Roman soldiers could achieve guarding the city of Philippi. Christians can live worry-free, but this is only possible when we lay our stresses and strains over to God. Grateful prayer is an antidote to worry.

Christians like the Philippians not only were to resist being conformed (8–9) to society. They could also redeem society by influencing it by the way they lived. In verses 8–9, Paul shows us that those experiencing the peace of God could proclaim the God of peace in a chaotic world. They would do so by *doing* what they learned, received, heard, and even saw in the example of Paul. Active Christians can be agents of change in society but we must first be reflective Christians. When Christians spend time meditating upon that which God says is true, respectable, just, pure, lovely, commendable, excellent, and praiseworthy then we develop a mindset through which to read, assess, process, and respond to society in a way that influences it for good. Only when believers know what have learned, received, heard, and seen in God's word can we identify what these great virtues are in daily life. We must tune into God's mind and heart and become the truth we embrace.

Thanksgiving and Closing words: In these last verses, Paul expresses his (10–2 gratitude for another financial gift he received from the Philippian believers. They had collaborated with him both while he was still in Macedonia and when he was beyond the boundaries of their region. As soon as the Philippians had opportunity to give, they did so because their caring for Paul never ceased. If in the past they had

42 Battle of Philippi   30 Soldiers colonize Philippi   Birth of Paul 4–6?

27 Caesar Augustus begins rule

stopped, it was because they lacked the opportunity to act on it. However, Paul was now under house arrest in Rome, and therefore a gift could be sent to a specific address. The Philippians did not miss the opportunity.

At this point Paul wants to qualify his position concerning their gift and take the opportunity to teach them a little bit about contentment in life, particularly with respect to money. Contentment did not hinge on having wealth. Paul had experienced the full spectrum of financial situations. He had lived with plenty and with nothing. From this, he learned that the secret of contentment is to lean on God. Money can be a competitor to God; it can deceive us into thinking that just a little more will satisfy. However, Paul reminds us twice that he had to learn through experience the secret of contentment. He too struggled, but in the end, he learned that all things can be done and all situations can be endured in the power of the strength of Christ. Only God satisfies. Of course, Paul was thanking the Philippians not because he wanted them to give more but because in giving they were involved in God's work. God would reward them because their gift was not motivated by a selfish gain but as an act of self-sacrificing worship. Paul knew that God would supply for their every need out of his unlimited wealth.

God always gives.[1] He uses believers to distribute his glorious riches, but we must always remember that he is the ultimate benefactor. Money may rest in believers' bank accounts but that does not mean it is theirs. Christians, rich or poor, are stewards of God's resources. They trust in him rather than their resources for their security, provision, and contentment in life. Rich and poor are all equally dependent on God. All that we have, give, and receive comes from God our father and only he deserves unending glory and our everlasting worship.

21–23) Paul ends the letter with several greetings and a blessing. As in his opening words, these closing thoughts reiterate that Christians are saints in the eyes of God. This is true because they stand before him by faith in Christ Jesus. Paul's final point is that Christian identity and standing before God is solely based on a relationship with Jesus. In his final words, greetings are sent to the Philippians from several groups. Among these, believers who are members of Caesar's household stand out. This is Paul's final way of calling the Philippian Christians to rejoice in the Lord even in a society that is loyal to *lord Caesar*. Some even in Caesar's household have turned to the Lord Jesus Christ! The gospel is advancing despite hardship and a final blessing completes the letter.

God versus Caesar

Roman Caesars were considered *Pater Patriae* meaning **Father of the Fatherland**. The title honored the emperor as the leader and gracious benefactor of all the blessings of living in his realm and under his rule. This was publicly advertised particularly in Rome and colony cities like Philippi. Though referring to God as *Father* is common in the Scriptures, the context of who ultimately is one's patron or benefactor in Philippians 4 would suggest there is irony in Paul's words. God, not Caesar is the real Father of the Philippian Christians despite what may be publicly exhibited in the theatres, streets, and public places of Philippi.

Res Gestae Divi Augusti

This is a fragment of *the Deeds of the Divine Augustus*. It was to be read following Caesar Augustus' death. In the 35th paragraph, Augustus indicates his status in the eyes of the Roman people as father of the nation.

Public Domain

---

1. Exodus 12:33–36; 15:25; 16:4–5; 1 Kings 17:2–6, 15–16; Romans 8:32

| 20 | 30 | 40 | 50 | 60 | 70 A.D. |

Jesus is crucified and resurrected 30–33?

Paul encounters Christ on Damascus road 33–34?

Paul's First Missionary Journey 46–47?

Paul's Second Missionary Journey 50–52?

Paul's first Roman imprisonment 60–62?

Paul's Caesarea imprisonment 58–60?

Paul's second Roman imprisonment and death 67?

119

Thanksgiving 1:3–11	Thanksgiving 4:10–20
Attitude of gratitude and contentment with reasons 1:3–11	Attitude of gratitude and contentment with reasons 4:10–20
Participation in the gospel from the first day (money) 1:5	Sharing in giving since beginning (money) 4:10, 15–16
Joy due to gift 1:3–4	Joy due to gift 4:10
God will complete work sanctification 1:6	God will reward expressions of sanctification 4:17b–18
Partner's in ministry 1:7	Share in ministry 4:14–16
Glory and praise of God 1:11	Glory to God our Father 4:20
Opening words 1:1–2	**Closing words 4:21–23**
Greeting 1:1–2	Greetings 4:21–23
Christ Jesus... the Lord Jesus Christ 1:1, 2	Christ Jesus... the Lord Jesus Christ 4:21, 23
All the saints 1:1	All the saints 4:21, 22
Grace 1:2	Grace 4:23

What is God saying?

We are now ready to summarize the discoveries we have made during the excavation of this passage. What is God teaching us through the words of the apostle Paul? In Philippians 1:1–16 Paul modeled the attitude and response to life that God wants all believers to exhibit. In Philippians 4:2–23, the

Where else is this taught in Scripture?

Priests Offering a Sacrifice
Throughout the Old Testament, God was very specific with the way that he was to be worshipped through sacrifices. Appropriate preparation is part of the process.

The life of sanctification encompasses the practical aspects of the Christian life in the midst of a godless world. In thanking the Philippians for their gift, Paul teaches us about money, giving, worship, contentment, and God. They are all related. Money may be a delicate topic to discuss, yet thankfully, we can learn about it with the help of Paul's *thank you* note. The apostle ties the sacrificial giving of money to the worship of God. In the Old Testament God showed his people how to worship him. This was crucial because it is only in worshipping God that contentment in life can be found. One of the established ways of worship was the offering of sacrifices. These were all costly expressions of faith and dependence upon God. It was an acknowledgement that life revolved around and depended upon him. The five main sacrifices in Leviticus 1–7 divided into two types: sweet smelling aromas pleasing to the Lord, and non-sweet smelling sacrifices. The fragrant offerings were presented as an act of love, devotion, and gratitude to God. They were a way of worshipping God and declaring, *in giving what costs me I show you I love and worship you*. This was a visual acknowledgement that satisfaction in daily life revolved around worshipping God. As the smoke of the sacrifice rose up in God's nostrils, he was pleased. The non-fragrant offerings, on the other hand, were apologies to God for sin. In our text, Paul uses the language of sacrifices of worship—sweet smelling aromas—to speak of financial giving in Philippians 4:18. This is because when they are offered sacrificially, worship rises up to God and delights him. Just as God gave Israel the opportunity to approach him on a daily basis and worship him, Christians today have that same opportunity albeit through different expressions. In Romans 12:1, it is the daily giving of one's life. In Philippians 4:18 it is the giving of money. However, just as in those days God's attention was focused on the heart of the giver not the size and quantity of the sacrifice, so it is for Christians today.

apostle directly applies this mindset. Believers today still struggle with one another when they let the world's values suppress God's truth. Christians need to learn how to respond to life's challenges within a world actively opposed to God. Lastly, believers need to learn about financial stewardship, gratitude, and contentment in life.

What God says through Paul concerning unity in the Lord, joy amidst hardship, gentleness in response to hostility, casting all our anxieties upon God, pursuing virtuous lives in keeping with truth, as well as issues of money, giving and contentment simply reiterates the teaching of the Lord Jesus Christ. Jesus prayed his followers would be united in their testimony to the world.[1] He also taught concerning joy in difficulty, gentleness, not worrying about life but trusting God, true godly living, the dangers of money, godly giving, and contentment in

Imperial Palace on the Palatine Hill
Think about the irony of how the gospel was advancing through Caesar's own staff as he contemplated what to do with Christians. His *household* would have referred to anyone from domestic slaves to high ranking civil servants.

Where else does this happen in history?

Count Nicolaus Ludwig von Zinzendorf was a German born into wealth and nobility in 1700. Raised by his Pietistic grandmother, Zinzendorf embraced the gospel at a very early age. By the age of ten, he had met the Savior and already decided the goal of his life: *I have but one passion—it is He [Christ], it is He alone. The world is the field and the field is the world; and henceforth that country shall be my home where I can be most used in winning souls for Christ.* Against the desires of his family, he committed his life and fortune to the cause of the gospel. The first step in this direction came providentially when Zinzendorf decided to buy his grandmother's estate in order to host families that were fleeing from religious persecution. This gave rise to the community of Herrnhut, meaning *the Lord's watch*. It would be the birthplace of the group known as the Moravians. In 1727, the community

Nicolaus Ludwig von Zinzendorf
Zinzendorf sacrificially used his wealth and nobility for the sake of the gospel. God used him to preach and reach people from nations around the world.

experienced a period of spiritual revival that resulted in a renewed commitment to the work of missions. Their first step was the establishment of a prayer vigil that continued around the clock, seven days a week, without interruption for more than one hundred years! In 1731, while visiting Copenhagen to attend the coronation of King Christian VI, Zinzendorf met a converted slave from the West Indies, Anthony Ulrich. This event prompted him to invite Ulrich to speak in Herrnhut and soon the community sent its first two missionaries to the Virgin Islands. After two decades they had send more missionaries around the globe than Protestants had sent in the past 200 years. There were missionaries sent to Greenland, Lapland, Georgia, Surinam, Africa's Guinea Coast, South Africa, Amsterdam's Jewish quarter, Algeria, the native North Americans, Ceylon, Romania, and Constantinople. Zinzendorf also authored many hymns and established a movement that efficiently endured the test of time. By the time of his death in 1760, the Moravians had successfully sent more than 220 missionaries worldwide. Zinzendorf was a worthy companion to men such as Paul, Timothy, and Epaphroditus, who gave all for the sake of Christ and the gospel.

1. John 17:20–23

God's will instead of possessions.[1] Therefore, Paul teaches believers about God's will for them as expressed in Christ.

What does God want?

God wants us to respond to what he says. There are many important principles of application in this passage so let's focus on just some of the major ones.

Stand united for Christ and dependent upon him

God wants us to get along. It is as simple as that. We owe it to him to put aside our differences and stand firm together. While there are some people you may struggle to see eye to eye with, you can still choose to get along. God also wants us to stand united in complete dependence upon him and not on our church, friends, position, or wealth. Life is hard. Difficulties come our way. Remember that God is greater than any of the stresses in life. He is available to you at every moment and situation. Isn't that remarkable? Entrust even the most seemingly insignificant situation into his care. God wants to be involved in the details of your life. He wants to be called into your hurts, worries, and fears. Let him in and enjoy his peace.

Learn to be content in God despite prosperity or poverty

Contentment in life does not depend on circumstances. This may be an easy truth to believe but living it is much more difficult. Most of us have grown to depend upon possessions, money, and comfort. We love these things. Though these are not wrong in and of themselves, they are unable to satisfy. How could they? Those made to enjoy God will only find joy in God. So learn to be content only in him and not in church, people, work, money, technology, or anything else. Be content in God alone.

Don't miss opportunities to give to God

God wants you to give financially to promote the progress of his kingdom. Collaborating with those in ministry is not just a privilege. It constitutes the worship of those who are growing in Christlikeness. Are you growing? God deserves your worship, and sacrificially letting go of money is a big statement of your desire to honor him as Lord of lords and King of kings. He knows the influence money has in your heart, and it is your heart and not your money which he desires exclusively for himself. Do not miss opportunities to give to Christian workers because they are everywhere and God is watching.

Give to Christian workers

Paul does not pause in Philippians to develop the topic of giving as he does in 1 Corinthians 9:3–15. There, Paul argues from Scripture that ministry workers are entitled to financial support from Christians. Paul often forfeited this right given the headaches it caused him from immature givers. It was simply easier at times to work to fund ministry himself. But the biblical principle remained: Christian workers are to be cared for by Christians. Entering ministry full time is a walk of faith, for those doing the work and those who are sacrificially supporting it.

Giving as Worship

The gift sent to Paul by the Philippians was deemed *a fragrant offering, an acceptable sacrifice, very pleasing to God.* This is the language used in the Old Testament to describe sacrifices pleasing to God. Paul connects giving with worship. When you give with the right motivation you ascribe greatness to God.

---

1. Matthew 5:17–7:29; 11:28–30; 26:39; Mark 12:28–34; Luke 12:15–21

Discoveries

Now that you have completed your seventh and final excavation into the rich soil of Philippians, it is time to stop digging and consider what you have learned. Choose the questions that are most helpful to you or your group.

Connecting with the community

These group questions are designed to help you apply what God wants from you. When applicable, think of these questions not only as an individual but also in terms of your family, your community, your nation, and your church.

1. Read Proverbs 15:1. How does this proverb apply to the conflict that Paul is addressing in Philippians 4:2–3? In what situations in your life could you benefit the most from the teaching of this verse? What events or relationships most provoke you to anger?

2. Philippians 4:2–3 describes a struggle between two members of the church. According to Paul, what was the solution to their disagreement? How can we apply this solution in our own churches today?

3. In Philippians 4:4–8, what is the relationship between the request to *rejoice* in verse 4 and the exhortations of verses 5–8?

4. Compile a list of things, activities, or ideas that you encounter in your daily life that would fit the description of: "*whatever is true, whatever is honorable, whatever is just, whatever is pure, whatever is lovely, whatever is commendable, if something is excellent or praiseworthy, think about these things.*" Why does Paul ask us to dwell on these things?

5. How is the Roman concept of peace or *pax romana* contrasted with the peace that God promises to believers? Can the world offer peace without the use of force? How is the difference between Roman peace and God's peace significant in our Christian walk?

6. In Philippians 4:11–13, Paul teaches his congregation about *contentment* in both prosperity and poverty. He then states that he can *do all things through him who strengthens me*. Why do we need God's strength in times of prosperity? Why do we need his strength in poverty? What does that teach us about God's strength?

7. What are the most common causes of worry in our society? How can Christians today fulfill the exhortation not to be anxious about anything? Suggest some practical ways in which this can be applied in your life.

8. What can we learn about having the generous heart of the Philippians? How is giving an expression of worship? What opportunities are available to you, to your family and to your church in giving to the Lord in your community and around the world?

9. Trace the argument of Philippians. How does Philippians 4:2–23 relate to the rest of the letter?

Probing deeper

These research exercises are for your continued study of Philippians in connecting key ideas with other Scripture. They require you to look at other passages beyond the text of Philippians and need to be thought of in terms of yourself, your family, your community, your nation, and your church.

1. Study 1 Chronicles 29:1–19. What can you learn from this passage regarding the topic of giving and its relationship to worship?

2. Meditate in the words of Christ in Matthew 6:19–34. How is this passage related to the issue of worry, particularly with regards to money, material possessions, and personal needs? In what areas of your life do you need to focus on God instead of worry?

3. In Philippians 4:2–3, Paul suggests resolution to a church problem by agreeing *in the Lord*. It is only the Lord who has the power strong enough to hold lasting reconciliation. In 1 Corinthians 12:12–27 Paul uses the analogy of the church as a body. How does this analogy help us with reconciliation within the church?

Bringing the story to life

Paul ties the giving of money to the worship of God giving several key principles that we can learn:

Notes, Observations & Questions

Principles of Giving in Philippians 4:10–20
- Giving to God's work is an ongoing responsibility.
- Giving to God's work is an opportunity not just a duty.
- God sends the opportunities to partner in giving.
- Giving is a self-sacrificial act of worship that costs us.
- Money is unnecessary for contentment in life.
- Money is unable to satisfy and competes with God to do so.
- God keeps track and rewards faithful stewards.
- God gives abundantly and he is the only real benefactor.

In 1 Corinthians 9:3–15 and 2 Corinthians 8–9 Paul provides additional teaching on giving:

Principles of Giving from 1 and 2 Corinthians
- Christians are to provide for Christian workers.
- Generosity does not depend on prosperity (2 Corinthians 8:2–3).
- Giving is a privilege to desire and excel in (2 Corinthians 8:4, 7; 9:2).
- Sacrificial giving is a Christ-like quality (2 Corinthians 8:9).
- Quality not quantity is the measure of giving (2 Corinthians 8:12).
- God watches the attitude of the giver (2 Corinthians 9:5b, 7).
- God rewards godly giving (2 Corinthians 9:6–11).
- Giving results in praise to God (2 Corinthians 9:12–15).

From these passages, create a presentation that can be made to your family, Sunday school class, church or other Christian group on Paul's teaching about giving. This presentation should include some or all the Scripture passages used. The purpose is to teach the biblical principles of giving so that people understand how our giving is a form of sacrificial worship to God.

Consider creative ways of presenting the material such as writing a skit where one character in the drama teaches a second character these principles. You can target your presentation for any age group you like. Once it is ready, you may want your pastor or another person with spiritual maturity to look over it before you present it.

Memorizing the key
Commit to memory the key phrase for Philippians 4:2–23, which is:
Dependence on Christ brings unity and contentment

Part of learning the Bible is remembering what the Bible is about and where to find things. Memorizing the key phrases will help you to better understand and apply the key points of each book.

Observation journaling
This section will help you review and remember the key verses in the book of Philippians. We have included three types of exercises: some for before you read, some for while you are reading, and some for after you have completed the reading.

Before you read
Review the entire book of Philippians in your own Bible. Write a single sentence to summarize each of the four chapters.
Summary sentence for chapter 1:

Summary sentence for chapter 2:

Summary sentence for chapter 3:

Summary sentence for chapter 4:

While you are reading
On the following page, we have laid out key verses from the book of Philippians with a wide margin so you can mark the text with questions, key terms, notes, and structures. Review the guidelines on *The art of active learning* section, page xi at the beginning of your *Field Notes* for some suggestions on reading, learning, and marking the text effectively.

.Key Philippian Passages

Philippians 1:6
For I am confident of this very thing, that he who began a good work in you will bring it to completion until the day of Christ Jesus.

Philippians 1:18
But what does it matter? Only that in every way, whether in pretense or in truth, Christ is proclaimed. And because of this I rejoice.

Philippians 1:21
For to me to live is Christ, and to die is gain.

Philippians 1:27a
Only live as citizens in a manner worthy of the gospel of Christ

Philippians 3:7–9
But whatever was to my profit I have come to regard as loss for the sake of Christ. More than that, I consider all things a loss compared to the far greater value of knowing Christ Jesus my Lord, for whom I have suffered the loss of all things—indeed I regard them as dung—that I may gain Christ and be found in him, not having a righteousness of my own that comes from the law, but that which is through faith in Christ Jesus, the righteousness from God that is by faith,

Philippians 3:20
But our citizenship is in heaven, and we await a savior from there, the Lord Jesus Christ,

Philippians 4:4–7
Rejoice in the Lord always. Again I say, rejoice! Let your gentleness be seen by all. The Lord is near! Do not be anxious about anything, but in everything by prayer and supplication, with thanksgiving, let your requests be made known to God. And the peace of God that surpasses all understanding will guard your hearts and your minds in Christ Jesus.

Notes, Observations & Questions

Summarize the text here

After you have read

1. Journaling is a great way to learn. By this point, you have hand written the entire book of Philippians. What have you learned so far from this ancient letter? This week, journal your thoughts as you consider God's message to the people of Philippi and what it means for us today. Write down how God wants you to respond to this letter and then take action accordingly.

2. Now read all of Philippians in your own Bible. Be sure you have reread the book completely before you begin the final *Field Study*. This will reinforce the learning of Scripture and help you retain it.

Pray

As we learn the Word of God, it is essential that we communicate with him through prayer. Commit to praying throughout the week alone or with others, asking God to help you identify areas in your life that distort his truth. Also, ask him to forgive you for doing so. Write your own prayer or use this as a sample prayer:

Dear God,

Thank you for letting me call upon you. I need you. Life has many difficulties but you are secure. I want to learn to rely on you. I want to learn to find contentment only in you. Help me Father to be content both in abundance or in need. Lead me to find my joy and security always in you rather than money or possessions. Change my heart and mind so that I become the joyful Christian you want me to be. Let my mind and my heart to be focused in all things good and godly. I want to be pleasing to you dear God. Help me to reach out to those with whom I struggle. Amen.

The Message
FIELD STUDY 9

We arrive at our final *Field Study* in Philippians. It is now time to step back and analyze our findings. We are finally ready to reflect on why God gave us this letter. Let's look at the contribution of Philippians to Scripture and history and discover its call on our lives today. It has much to say about displaying God in godless times.

What is the contribution to the Scriptures?
From Genesis to Revelation: The story of history

Living for God in a world ruled by Satan brings tension. Nevertheless, it is God's will that we live exclusively for him. Many have done so before us blazing a trail so that we may follow their example. Let's revisit the story of mankind through the eyes of Scripture and learn from others who have conformed to the likeness of God rather than the pattern of this world.

The climax of the creation account in Genesis was the formation of a being in the very image and likeness of God. Consider it for a moment. God created Adam and Eve to be like him. Man and woman were to be his representatives on earth.[1] The world was to be, and once was, a God-honoring realm—a heaven on earth. God's image-bearers were to rule over his creation in harmony and in relationship with him, multiplying in number so that the earth would be filled with God's representatives. However, Adam and Eve's rebellion placed the world under their mediated care to Satan. The world was now controlled by the evil influence of God's angelic enemy. This resulted in disunity, tension and

The World God Created
We often do not see our world through spiritual eyes of good and evil. Yet, God has created it and is redeeming it from the rule of Satan. Living on earth as a believer brings great tension.

1. Genesis 1:26–28

Apollo 17, 1972

The Garden of Eden

The Garden of Eden was a place where the goal of God for creation could be seen. It was a place of peace, beauty, abundance, and harmony where mankind could rule the earth while enjoying perfect immediate fellowship with God without the effects of sin.

Thomas Cole, 1828

a god-defying mindset that became the norm. Earth was no longer a heavenly place. Though created to display God's glory and enjoy fellowship with him, mankind chose to live in rebellion to his gracious Creator.

God did not allow his image to remain marred without reprisal nor would he allow mankind to remain hopelessly lost. He promised to bless the nations through a descendant of Eve, and later Abraham. A descendent whom we now know was the Lord Jesus Christ.[1] Yet, despite God's gracious and personal commitment to undo the intrusion of evil on his earth, primeval mankind—just like today—repeatedly rejected God's provision to receive and enjoy life in fellowship with him. Some, however, had the courage to stand out for God despite the pressures of the society in which they lived. Enoch walked with God;[2] likewise, Noah and his family put up with the scorn of an unbelieving society for many years for the sake of living God's way.[3] Society may have become unrepresentative of God, but God graciously and faithfully worked with and through those who chose to live as his representative citizens on earth.

> ## Genesis 3:15
>
> And I will put enmity between you and the woman, and between your offspring and her offspring; he will bruise your head and you will strike his heel.

> ## Genesis 50:19–20
>
> But Joseph said to them, do not be afraid. Am I in the place of God? As for you, you meant to harm me, but God meant it for good, to preserve many lives, as they are today.

Out of the context of man's further flagrant rebellion toward God at the tower of Babel, God called a man and his family to serve in the outworking of his redemptive plans. The family of Abraham, Isaac, and Jacob constitutes the lineage of the patriarchs who bore God's promised solution for humanity. Nevertheless, they also fell prey to the pressures of society to conform, grab, cheat, lie, and compromise. But once again, one man from Abraham's family stood out in that time for his unwavering commitment to God in the midst of a godless society and personal disappointments. The story of Joseph is filled with jealousy, cruelty, injustice, sorrow, and temptation. However, in spite of these trials, Joseph was able to break the pattern of the story of Genesis in that he was completely committed and obedient to his God. Joseph showed the world that God is worth loving, obeying, and displaying in life even when things do not go our way.

1. Genesis 22:14
2. Genesis 5:21–24
3. Genesis 6:8–9, 22; 7:5

B.C. 2000	1850	1700	1550	1400	1250

2091 God calls Abraham?

1925 God calls Abraham?

Receiving the Law on Mount Sinai? 1446

Receiving the Law on Mount Sinai? 1260

Good Kings of Judah

King	Year	Reign	Character
Asa	911–870	41 years	Good
Jehoshaphat	870–848*	25 years	Good
Joash	835–796	40 years	Good
Amaziah	796–767	29 years	Good
Uzziah (Azariah)	767–740*	52 years	Good
Jotham	740–732*	16 years	Good
Hezekiah	716–687	29 years	Good
Josiah	640–608	31 years	Good

The story of mankind moves to the nation of Israel who was appointed as God's representative nation among all of the peoples of the world. God wanted Israel to display him before all nations, showing the world that being a citizen in a nation ruled by God was the best possible option for life on earth. For this reason, God called Israel to be different, set apart, or holy. *"Be Holy for I am holy"* was God's call to those who would represent him.[4] Israel was a nation of redeemed image-bearers worthy of living as citizens under God's sovereign rule.

There was still the continued tendency to compromise and assimilate into the nations of the earth rather than standout as godly citizens. However, there are examples in every stage of Israel's history that show the watching world that it is possible to live displaying the values of God in a pagan society. In the times of the exodus and the conquest of the Promised Land, we see people like Moses, Joshua, and Caleb who lived according to the Law of God despite the path of the masses. In the period of the Judges generations of God's people ignored his will and values as expressed in the Law, but there were also individuals like Ruth and Boaz who lived self-sacrificially in obedience

Ruth and Boaz
In the book of Ruth, obedience to God is presented in the relationships between Naomi, Ruth, and Boaz. All three depict God's loving-kindness toward his people.

Barent Fabritius, 1660

Victory over the Amalekites
In Exodus 17:8–16, Moses called Joshua to lead the fight against the Amalekites. Moses stood on top of a hill with the staff of God in his hand and God blessed the Israelite's obedience and gave them victory.

Joshua 24:15

But if you have no desire to serve the LORD, choose for yourselves today whom you will serve, whether the gods your fathers served beyond the River, or the gods of the Amorites in whose land you are living. But as for me and my house, we will serve the LORD.

Nicolas Poussin, 1625

4. Leviticus 11:45

1250   1100   950   800   650   500   B.C.

Saul becomes king 1050
David becomes king 1010
Solomon becomes king 971
930 The kingdom divides
722 Northern kingdom falls to Assyria
Southern kingdom falls to Babylon and the temple is destroyed 586

131

Daniel's Answer to the King

The jealousy and envy of the leaders of Babylon caused Daniel to be thrown into the lion's den, but not even this was able to move him from his devotion to the one true God. After an entire night among lions, he testified to the king that God protected him (Daniel 6:22).

Britton Rivière, 1890

to God for the sake of others. The period of the monarchy also provides rare glimpses of kings who countered the values of their wicked generations to conform to the Law of God. Countless prophets also stood strong for God amidst trials and tribulations. There were also men like Daniel and his three friends Hananiah, Mishael, and Azariah who chose to live without compromise while exiled in a culture where even their lives were at stake.[1] After the return from exile, individuals like Zerubbabel, Ezra, and Nehemiah lived in conformity to God despite the taunts and disappointments of the society around them.[2] Finally, John the Baptist at the end of the Old Testament age stood as a bold, counter-cultural, humble representative of God.[3] History shows that God *can be* represented on hostile terrain.

> ## Daniel 1:8
>
> But Daniel resolved that we would not defile himself with the king's food and wine, and he asked the commander of the officials to allow him not to defile himself.

Then God himself came to earth in the person of Jesus Christ, and showed the world that the Father can be obediently represented despite the pressures to compromise. For this reason, only Christ's perfect sacrifice provides the way to fellowship with God through faith in him.[4] According to the Scriptures, those who believe in Christ are still responsible to live in this age as his representatives and not in love with the things and ways of this world.[5] The call of God to *"Be holy because I am holy"* remains. Imitating him is still the privilege and responsibility of those who have

> ## John 3:30
>
> He must increase, But I must decrease.

Philips Augustijn Immenraet, 1663

The Temptation of Christ

At the beginning of his ministry, Jesus was led by the Spirit into the desert to be tempted by the devil. After forty days of fasting, Jesus resisted the temptations of Satan and modeled perfect godly obedience.

1. Daniel 1:8; 3:1–30; 6:1–28
2. Ezra 4:1–5; Nehemiah 4:1–23
3. John 3:22–36; Matthew 3:1–17
4. Hebrews 9:1–28
5. James 4:4; Proverbs 4:14–15

B.C.	1	A.D.	10	20	30	40	50

5? Birth of Jesus

4–6? Birth of Paul

John the Baptist begins his ministry 28–29?

Jesus begins his ministry 28–30?

Jesus is crucified and resurrected 30–33?

33–34? Paul encounters Christ on Damascus road

46–47? First Missionary Journey by Paul

embraced the gospel of Jesus Christ. However, the world and its governing standards do not seek to be colonized by heavenly citizens; it constantly fights back hard in return, just as Jesus has warned those who followed him.

> f the world hates you, know that it has hated me first. If you belonged to the world, the world would love you as its own; but because you are not of the world, but I chose you out of the world, for this reason the world hates you. Remember what I told you, 'A servant is not greater than his master.' If they persecuted me, they will also persecute you. If they obeyed my word, they will obey yours also. But all these things they will do to you because of my name, because they do not know the One who sent me.

John 15:18–21

This will be the case until Christ returns.[6] Therefore, God's people can expect that tension and strain will persist throughout their lives.[7]

From beginning to end, the story of mankind is about God receiving the glory he alone deserves through the restoration of a rebellious creation back to himself. In redeeming rebellious image-bearers through the gospel of Jesus Christ, God displays his unrivalled glory. Until all is restored and renewed under Christ in the end, tension remains for his people living for him in a fallen realm. The pressures to embrace the self-seeking values of a godless culture and be absorbed into the pattern of a society opposed to godly living remain strong. Living for God in Satan's domain will continue to be a struggle, and yet God deserves our lives lived exclusively for him. After all, this earth will not be Satan's realm forever.

The Contribution of Philippians

Philippians is perhaps the most affectionate and practical of all of the letters Paul wrote to churches. It is not unique in the truth it proclaims, but it is distinct in the angle and lens through which it helps the reader understand the grand biblical narrative in a more focused and practical way. It invokes concepts such as *citizenship* and the use of *role models*. So why did God allow this book to be included in the Bible? What role does it play? Let's examine three specific or unique contributions Philippians makes.

The first contribution this letter makes to our Christian faith is to demonstrate that *the advance of the gospel of Jesus Christ is unstoppable.* Prison chains, house arrest, soldiers, Caesars, societal pressure,

Imitatio

Imitating role models was an ancient and effective practice. The ancient writer Seneca said it well when he declared: *"Let us choose, however, from among the living... men who teach us by their lives, men who tell us what we ought to do and then prove it by practice, who show us what we should avoid, and then are never caught doing that which they have ordered us to avoid."*
(Epistle 52.8 translated by Richard M. Gummere, Loeb Classical Library)

God too wants Christians to imitate the right role models.

6. Revelation 20:7–9
7. 1 Peter 1:6–9; 2 Timothy 3:1–5

| 50 | 60 | 70 | 80 | 90 | 100 A.D. |

49? Jerusalem Council

60–62? Paul arrives in Rome under house arrest

70 Temple is destroyed

John writes Revelation 95–96?

50–52? Second Missionary Journey by Paul

64 Fire in Rome

79 Pompeii and Herculaneum are destroyed by Vesuvius eruption

133

Carmen Christi?

Why is the *Hymn of Christ* or in Latin, *Carmen Christi* not a contribution of Philippians singled out here? The Christ Hymn presented in Philippians 2:6–11 is an insight into the praise of the early church and contains wonderful truths concerning the Lord Jesus Christ. The reason Paul invokes it, however, is not primarily to present Christology—teaching concerning Christ—but to present the attitude of Christ as a role model to imitate.

Revisiting the Outline

Ancient writers often used writing techniques to highlight sections of their writings. One tool at their disposal was modeled after the Greek letter X called a chiasm. Chiasms vary greatly but essentially show emphasis through structure. Look at how Philippians returns to how it started and in doing so emphasizes the central section. It's like the central appeal is the tip of an arrow.

Opening words 1:1–2
  Expression of Thanksgiving and Prayer 1:3–11
    Paul's Situation 1:12–26
      Central Appeal with Examples 1:27–4:1
    Philippian Situation 4:2–9
  Expression of Thanksgiving 4:10–20
Closing Words 4:21–23

and adverse circumstances cannot stop the progress of the gospel. Christ is proclaimed even through the selfish interests of his people! Philippians shows us that God's purposes in history cannot be stopped by the taunts and frowns of society. We are called to evangelize, which God himself empowers. Salvation, from beginning to end, belongs to him and his offer of salvation to the nations will advance regardless of opposition. In the end, every human being will recognize, on bended knee that Jesus Christ is Lord. Even those who have rejected Christ will bow when his full glory is revealed. The gospel will progress.

Philippians makes a second contribution to our understanding of reality. While Paul presents the gospel in books like Galatians and Romans, he makes a special emphasis on the *demands of* the gospel makes on those who believe. This letter makes a huge contribution to our understanding of discipleship. It addresses the meaning of following Christ in everyday life. It reminds us that *the gospel is not just a truth to believe but also a truth to incarnate.* The gospel is about justification and sanctification because it makes practical claims on the daily life of people. God wants Christians to develop a certain mindset through which to assess the world and embrace his values. He wants Christians to exhibit an attitude of joy, humility, self-sacrifice, perseverance, and boldness, which goes against the values of the world. God wants believers to behave in unity and partnership, even in the midst of suffering, as an expression of the effects of the gospel in their lives. Such unity is also a proclamation of the gospel God offers to the watching world. Believers who live out the demands of the gospel serve as an advertisement of the gospel.

Lastly, the book of Philippians is distinct in the practical way in which it shows Christians *how to live as heavenly citizens* on earth through the example of role models. In Philippians, we get to see how to live for Christ in a hostile society. The letter reminds us of the value of mentoring within the Christian community. Just as Joshua had Moses, Elisha had Elijah, and Timothy had Paul, Christians today have all of these biblical characters and ultimately Christ himself as worthy models for our behavior. As believers display God's will on earth, they do so in a counter-cultural way. The way of the world is not the way of Christ and compromise or blending in, is not an option. We must portray the heavenly

Ephesians 5:1–2

Therefore, be imitators of God as dearly loved children and walk in love, just as Christ loved us and gave himself up for us, a fragrant offering and sacrifice to God.

B.C.	1	A.D.	10	20	30	40	50

5? Birth of Jesus

4–6? Birth of Paul

John the Baptist begins his ministry 28–29?

Jesus begins his ministry 28–30?

Jesus is crucified and resurrected 30–33?

33–34? Paul encounters Christ on Damascus road

46–47? First Missionary Journey by Paul

values of God's kingdom before a crooked and perverse society. Heavenly citizens are imitators of God enslaved to their role model Jesus Christ. Philippians helps us see how to be like Jesus Christ.

How did it end?

What happened when the Philippians received this letter? What happened to the Philippian church beyond the lifetime of Paul, Timothy, and Epaphroditus? Is there a church in Philippi today?

Thomas Cole, 1836

The Course of Empire Destruction
The great fire of Rome began on July 19, A.D. 64 and according to Roman historian Tacitus, it burned for six days.

We do not know how the Philippian church responded to Paul's letter. There is no reason to doubt a positive response. Paul was probably released from house arrest in Rome and eventually visited Philippi. The book of Acts does not record this because it ends with Paul under arrest in Rome prior to his audience with Caesar. Given that in Acts, the Roman authorities see no reason to find Paul guilty,[1] it is likely that Paul's confidence in being released and visiting the Philippians became a reality.[2] Upon release, Paul continued to minister among the churches and probably travelled to Philippi and Thessalonica. He also wrote at least three other letters: 1 Timothy, 2 Timothy, and Titus. Timothy became the pastor of the church in Ephesus, which is where he was when Paul wrote the letters bearing his name. Tradition holds that Timothy died in A.D. 97 at the hands of a mob who stoned him for preaching the gospel while trying to stop a pagan idolatrous procession. We do not know what became of Epaphroditus once he returned to his home fellowship in Philippi.

The history of Christianity in Philippi continues past the first century. In the early years of the second century A.D., the bishop of Antioch named Ignatius passed through Philippi on the *Via Egnatia* as a prisoner on route to Rome to be thrown to wild beasts. The Christians there took care of him. Then, the Philippian believers wrote

Did Paul Die in Rome?

What happened between Paul's release in A.D. 62 and his imprisonment again and death as testified in 2 Timothy? It seems the burning of Rome changed things for Christians in A.D. 64. It is possible Nero started the fire to create space in Rome for a new palace. When Romans began to accuse him of this, Nero found an easy scapegoat in Christians. Alternatively, the fire may have been an accident, but Nero still accused Christians to divert any unfair accusations. Either way, the Christians were blamed. The result was that when Christian leaders like Peter and Paul were caught, they were martyred. According to church tradition, Paul was beheaded by Nero in Rome.

1. Acts 25:26–27; 26:31–32
2. Philippians 1:23–25; 2:24

| 50 | 60 | 70 | 80 | 90 | 100 A.D. |

49? Jerusalem Council

50–52? Second Missionary Journey by Paul

60–62? Paul arrives in Rome under house arrest

64 Fire in Rome

70 Temple is destroyed

79 Pompeii and Herculaneum are destroyed by Vesuvius eruption

John writes Revelation 95–96?

135

Remnants of a Basilica in Philippi

Even today, it is easy to see the remains of the Christian community in Philippi. These archaeological ruins are from one of the churches built in Philippi.

to Polycarp, bishop of Smyrna and friend of Ignatius, asking him to send them any writings Ignatius had written. Polycarp responds with his own *Letter to the Philippians*, which exists to this day. Polycarp's words suggest that this next generation of Christians were still undergoing similar oppression.

Numerous churches were built in Philippi between the late 4th and into the 6th century A.D. One of these was the famous basilica of Paul. In this church, a floor mosaic from the 4th century was found with an inscription by Bishop Porphyrios who was one of a series of Philippian bishops to have attended the church councils of Sardica (A.D. 344), Ephesus (A.D. 431), and Chalcedon (A.D. 451). Clearly, Christianity remained strong and vibrant in Philippi long after Paul, Euodia, Syntyche, Epaphroditus, and Clement.

From the late sixth century on, Philippi slowly lost economic importance while at the same time, gaining strategic and military significance. It attracted a series of armies with expansionist dreams driving people away to safer lands. For centuries, Philippi was a military outpost for the Slavs, Byzantines, Bulgars, Franks, Serbs, and Turks until it was finally abandoned at an unknown date and left as a heap of ruins, which remain even today.

Mosaic on the Floor of Paul's Basilica

This mosaic on the floor of Paul's Basilica in Philippi dates back to around A.D. 343. The inscription reads, *Porphyrios, bishop, made the mosaic floor of the basilica of Paul in Christ.*

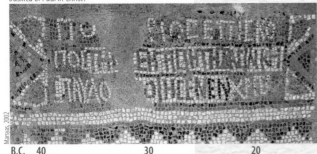

What does this have to do with Jesus?

There are over fifty references to Jesus in Philippians, so there can be no doubt it is a Christ-centered letter. Our textual excavations have revealed this. Everything Paul writes flows out of his revelation about the Lord Jesus Christ. So let's summarize what Paul says, and

| B.C. 40 | 30 | 20 | 10 | B.C. 1 A.D. | 10 |

42 Battle of Philippi

30 Soldiers colonize Philippi

27 Caesar Augustus begins rule

Birth of Paul 4–6?

136

in doing so, highlight what Philippians tells us about Christ.

- Jesus is God in human form (2:6–8)
- Jesus Christ alone is Lord despite the claims of many human rulers—like Caesar—and the words of his many enemies (1:2, 14; 2:11, 19; 3:18, 20; 4:1)
- The primary identity of Christians and our only position as saints before God is found in Jesus Christ (1:1; 3:9, 14; 4:23)
- Jesus is the one through whom believers can experience: joy (1:26; 3:1; 4:4, 10), unity (4:2), peace (4:7), strength (4:13), God's rich supplies (4:19), a genuine reason to boast (3:3), and spiritual growth (1:11)
- Jesus reveals to us that God self-sacrificially gives of himself to be available to man (2:5–8; 4:5)
- Jesus Christ is our greatest role model in values, attitude, and behavior for godly living in a hostile world (1:8; 2:5–11)
- Jesus is the authority to whom believers will render an account of their lives on the Day of Christ (1:6, 10; 2:16)
- Jesus Christ is the greatest authority over all things and all of mankind will recognize this one day (2:9–11)
- A personal relationship with Jesus Christ is the goal of life and so proclaiming him at all costs is our ultimate Christian duty and privilege in life (1:13, 15, 17, 18, 20, 21, 27, 29; 2:30; 3:7–11)

What does God want?

Our exploration of Philippians comes to an end. Throughout this exploration and discovery, God challenged us in many ways. Here is a final opportunity to respond to him. Take time to consider these important areas of application to your life. Remember to keep this question always in mind: what does God want me to do?

Live to display God in your everyday world

We all live in a wicked and crooked generation. Hostility toward God is not always flagrant but it is opposition nonetheless. God calls us to be lights within the darkness even if it means being mocked and scorned. Through the centuries, many believers around the world have been persecuted and opposed for their faith. That oppression continues to this day. Our world needs to see God on display. They must see who God is, what he is like, and what he values through the way we think, act, and interact in life. This is the privilege and responsibility of heavenly citizens. There is a reason that God still has us on the earth. He deserves our bold, counter-cultural, self-sacrificing, and humble representation. Displaying him through a worthy walk with Christ may not advance you in the eyes of the

Polycarp's Letter

In the early second century A.D., Polycarp wrote to believers in Philippi. His letter echoes the themes of Paul's letter. Polycarp encourages the next generation of Philippian Christians to a worthy walk in the midst of persecution, to the imitation of Christ and other noble Christians, to remember the judgment seat of Christ, to unity and gentleness, and to the dangers of the love of money.

Public Domain

The Roman Fasces

The Roman fasces was a bundle of wooden rods tied with a rope with a protruding axe head. It represented the strength of power and authority accomplished through unity in the Roman world. Despite associations today, in the first century A.D. this symbol represented the greatness of the Roman commonwealth of which every Roman citizen was proud to be a member. United, citizens of Rome could rule with power and authority.

| 20 | 30 | 40 | 50 | 60 | 70 A.D. |

Jesus is crucified and resurrected 30–33?

Paul's First Missionary Journey 46–47?

Paul's first Roman imprisonment 60–62?

Paul encounters Christ on Damascus road 33–34?

Paul's Caesarea imprisonment 58–60?

Paul's Second Missionary Journey 50–52?

Paul's second Roman imprisonment and death 67?

Philippians 2:9–11

Therefore, God highly exalted him and gave him the name that is above every name, so that at the name of Jesus every knee will bow—in heaven and on earth and under the earth—and every tongue confess that Jesus Christ is Lord, to the glory of God the Father.

world. We have all been warned through Philippians, so we can expect struggle and rejection. Yet, we have the privilege to exhibit God in our society today. We must find ways to do so.

Let godly influences shape you

Society does a good job of marketing itself upon us. If we are to display God in a counter-cultural way, we need to be proactive in response. How can our lives be shaped to boldly advertise God? How do we become more like Christ? The Holy Spirit has many ways of accomplishing this. Consider the following two. *Studying and applying the Scriptures* submits us to an influence that shapes our thinking and worldview. We must begin to see the world through God's eyes. *Meaningful relationships with godly people* will also shape and equip us to live for Christ. Do you have godly role models? Can you pursue a relationship with one? We all become like that which we admire, imitate, interact, and allow into our lives. We can only display God, as he desires, when he is transforming us on a daily basis. We all need a little bit of help every day. Rather than giving in to society, let godly influences shape you. Find those who walk in close fellowship with Jesus and join them. Then find someone who you can influence, mentor, and lead into a deeper relationship with Christ.

Philippi Today

The remains of some of the structures that stood when Paul and Silas first visited Philippi can still be seen today.

Todd Bolen, www.BiblePlaces.com

Discoveries

Now that you have completed the analysis of the entire book of Philippians, it is time to consider what you have learned and the difference it can make in your life. Choose the questions that are most helpful to you or your group.

Connecting with the community

These group questions are designed to help you apply what God wants from you. When applicable, think of these questions not only as an individual but also in terms of your family, your community, your nation, and your church.

1. What is the contribution of Philippians to the overall story of the Bible?

2. What was the most critical issue that caused disunity in the church of Philippi? Could you identify the issue that is most disruptive to the unity of the members of your group or church? Is there something you can learn from this book regarding that issue?

3. Who were the Judaizers? How did their interpretation of the Old Testament and the law destroy the sufficiency of the message of the gospel? Are there any *Judaizers* in your church? What is it that they are seeking to add to the gospel?

4. Read the entire letter of Philippians one more time and look for the following concepts: joy, citizenship, unity, humility, perseverance, self-sacrifice, suffering, and boldness. What is the relationship that exists between these concepts?

5. Based on your study and analysis of the main concepts taught in this epistle, how would you summarize the concept of sanctification? What are its essential components? Use several verses from the letter to the Philippians as the basis of your summary.

6. How does the message of Philippians reveal the person of Christ?

Notes, Observations & Questions

7. What does the book of Philippians teach us about the character of God? Think about this issue in the context of the importance that Philippians gives to the concept of citizenship and to the relationship of the believer to God in Christ.

8. Based on what you have learned from the book of Philippians, what is the relationship that exists between suffering and faithfulness to the cause of Christ? According to Philippians, how does suffering fit in the daily life of the believer?

9. Is the purpose of the gospel merely to justify sinners? That is, does God merely seek to grant justification to those who believe? Defend your answer from the teaching of Philippians.

10. Why will people who truly live as a faithful citizens of heaven encounter opposition from society?

11. What image or artifact would best represent the book of Philippians? For example, we could say that Philippians is like taking a fitness test, which allows us to see how healthy and strong our commitment is to Christ and his cause. You could also represent the book using a different image or creature. What would you pick?

12. On a scale of 1 to 10 with 1 representing a little and 10 representing a lot, rate again your knowledge of the book of Philippians. Did it improve over the course of this study? What will stand out in your mind one year from now when you think of the message of Philippians?

1   2   3   4   5   6   7   8   9   10
a little   a lot

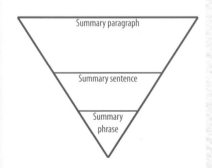

Summary paragraph

Summary sentence

Summary phrase

13. Learning how to summarize new information is a very important skill. Summarizing helps you to catch the essence of meaning from the text. Now that you have completed the study of the book of Philippians, enlarge the triangle chart that you see on the left. Fill it first with a summary paragraph of all of Philippians. Then narrow it into a summary sentence and finally narrow it into a phrase. Have you captured the intention of the apostle Paul?

14. Now that you have summarized Philippians, it is important that you remember how this ancient letter fits in with the rest of Scripture. Create a large version of the chart on the right. The main topic is the message of Philippians. In the large box, fill in all the relevant information about the message of Philippians. Then in the largest box, tell how the message of Philippians fits into the story of Scripture. How does the book contribute to our understanding and proclamation of the gospel? In what sense is Christ the fulfillment of the message of this book? This will help you remember how Philippians contributes to the story of Scripture.

> What does Philippians teach us about the gospel of Jesus Christ?
>
> > What do I know about Philippians?
> >
> > > The message of Philippians

Probing deeper

These exercises are for your continued study of Scripture and go beyond the text of Philippians. These exercises trace themes found in Philippians through other parts of Scripture and need to be thought of in terms of yourself, your family, your community, your nation, and your church.

Notes, Observations & Questions

1. Go back to page 14 of the *Discoveries* section of *Field Study 1* and complete your prediction chart by writing the actual problem in the Philippian church. Was it what you expected? Does this teach you anything about how God works?

2. Why was it important for the apostle Paul to express his joy in the midst of his difficult circumstances? Discuss how the church in the present can encourage its members to rejoice in the Lord always. What is the source of enduring joy for the believer?

3. Consider the attitude of Christ and the degree to which he was willing to humble himself. Compare this attitude to that of your church or denomination. Is humility an important value and a trait in your church? If not, what can you do to improve in this area?

4. Read and prayerfully meditate on Isaiah 53:1–12. Can you describe in your own words the way in which the book of Philippians is an extended proclamation of the truth of this passage from the book of Isaiah? Write a prayer, poem, or song giving glory to God and expressing your gratitude to Jesus for his gracious and loving work on your behalf. Follow the pattern of Philippians 2:5–11, giving glory to God because of the true gospel.

5. Write down five major lessons you have learned throughout the course of this study. For each thing that you have learned, describe at least one practical implication that such teaching will have in your daily life.

6. How would you start a conversation about the gospel with an unbeliever using the book of Philippians? Write down a paragraph that would show the beginning of your conversation. Start the paragraph with the message of Philippians and connect it to the person and work of Christ.

Bringing the story to life

Now that you have read the entire book of Philippians, it is important to teach this book to someone else. This is one of the most effective forms of learning. It may be that you want to work through it with a friend or a family member, one on one. You may want to teach Philippians in your church or Bible study group. You could set up a Bible study in your community or create an after school program for young adults. You may teach children at Sunday school or even your own kids at home.

How could you creatively communicate God's message? Could you use a picture, a logo, a song, or a rhyme? Is there an object or illustration that would help to communicate the message? It is very important that you plan your lessons. What concepts do you want your students to understand? What themes in Philippians will you teach? Once you are ready, try it out.

Memorizing the key

Commit to memory the key phrase for the entire book of Philippians. The key phrase for Philippians is:

<blockquote>Godly living displays God to a needy world</blockquote>

Go back and review all nine key phrases. The key phrases represent the basic message of the book in each section. They are meant to be reminders of the content of the letter to the Philippians. If you have taken the time to memorize the key phrases in order, then you will know the basic flow and message of the book of Philippians. If you do this with multiple books in the Bible, you will be able to recall quickly where the biblical authors address the various issues of Scripture.

Observation journaling

Developing a habit of writing what you have studied is a very helpful part of learning. Now, it is important for you to read Philippians in your own Bible and mark the key structures, terms, and meaning of each section. By transferring to your Bible what you have learned in this study, you will always be able to review what you have learned regarding the meaning of the text and its application. The process will also reinforce what you have learned. If you do not like to write in your Bible, create a piece of paper that you can insert and keep in your Bible. Consider the following practices anytime you read God's Word:

Before you read

Always work at linking information that you already know with what you are learning. Anytime you come to a passage, review the context, the author, and any other information you might already know to prepare you to learn more.

While you are reading

Every time you read the biblical text, mark the text with questions, key terms, notes, and structures. Keep in mind the guidelines on *the art of active learning* section, page xi at the beginning of your *Field Notes* to create a habit of active reading, learning and marking the text effectively.

After you have read

As soon as you have finished reading, write down any questions that you may have that were not answered in Philippians. Why do you think God left those questions unanswered? Are they answered in other parts of Scripture? Create a journal that records your thoughts about what you are learning. Be sure to continue to review and reread in order to master the material.

Pray

Write a prayer, psalm, or poem to God capturing his message in Philippians. What does it mean to live as citizens of heaven? Pray for the effect of the gospel on the worldwide Church, your local church, nation, community, family, and yourself. We have provided a sample prayer on the following page. Use it as a guide for your own prayer.

Notes, Observations & Questions

Dear Heavenly Father,

Thank you God for the book of Philippians and the contribution it makes to the overall story of Scripture. This letter written by Paul long ago is so relevant for my life and the life of my church. Just like the first century believers, I too live under the pressure of a culture that is hostile towards you. Please forgive me Lord of often conforming myself to the pattern of this world rather than standing out the way I should as a Christian. Help me grow in boldness for Christ as I purposefully live a counter-cultural life. I pray that I would model my life and behavior after people like Paul and Timothy but mostly your Son, Jesus Christ. I pray that my joy will come not from my fleeting circumstances, but through the eternal hope I have in your exaltation in the world and living with you in eternity. I thank you Lord that everyone will bow the knee and confess you as Lord one day. Make yourself Lord of my life today. I pray in your most wonderful and exalted name, Jesus. Amen.

Glossary

Term	Definition
Apostle	An apostle is "one sent out to proclaim a message." In the Bible, it refers to a special messenger from God. The apostles were charged with the duty to proclaim the message of the gospel and its implications for life.
Asia Minor	The ancient region of the Roman Empire roughly located in the same territory of modern day Turkey.
Book of Life	In the context of Paul's concept of heavenly citizenship, this book refers to a metaphorical heavenly register in which the names of believers are written.
Christ	Title of the Anointed One who was to come and bring deliverance. The term is synonymous with Messiah. Christians believe that the Messiah/Christ is Jesus. The belief is reflected in the constant usage of the title Jesus Christ in the New Testament.
Christian	A name given to a person who believes in Jesus Christ, the Son of God is the redeemer of mankind. The term was first applied to the disciples in Antioch of Syria after Paul and Barnabas had taught there for about one year. See Acts 11:26.
Christology	The study of the person and work of Jesus Christ. It includes the study of Jesus as the Messiah and the Son of God.
Circumcision	The God-ordained act of cutting off the male foreskin as a sign of membership in the people of Israel. Given to Abraham in Genesis 17.
Citizenship (Roman; Heavenly)	A privileged status of belonging to a country or realm that carries with it a responsibility to display the values and greatness of it.
Declaration of Chalcedon	The declaration that contains the summary of the decisions of the Council of Chalcedon (A.D. 451) regarding the Person of Christ and the nature of the union of his divine and human natures.
Discipleship	The growth in holiness and Christ-likeness of a follower of Jesus Christ.
Epaphroditus	A believer from the city of Philippi chosen by the community to travel to Rome to minister to Paul. The apostle Paul presents him as a living example of Christ-like character worthy of imitating.
Eschatology	The study of end time events such as the second coming of Christ, the tribulation, the millennium and the final judgment.
Exordium	That portion of ancient speeches where the topic is previewed and rapport is built with the audience.
Glorification	The final consummation of Christian salvation. God's promise of salvation in the Bible will reach its climax when a believer's transformation from sinfulness to righteousness is finally complete. It will only happen after the resurrection when the Christian is in the presence of God.
Gospel	The phrase literally means "good news." It can be used in several ways. In general, the gospel is that eternal life with God is available again. Specifically, the gospel refers to the basis upon which eternal life with God is made available, that is, the death and resurrection of Jesus Christ. At times the term is also used to refer to the New Testament books of Matthew, Mark, Luke, and John—the Gospels.
Grace	In simple terms, grace is an unmerited favor. In the Bible, grace is the foundation upon which God offers salvation to mankind. Salvation is therefore an undeserved gift, bestowed by God upon anyone who believes in the gospel of Christ.
Imitatio	The concept of learning by copying or imitating the lifestyle and beliefs of a person who you follow as a disciple.

Term	Definition
Jesus Christ	The Son of God. The second person of the Trinity. The God-man born of the virgin Mary, who for us and for our salvation became human, suffered, died, and rose again from the grave to free his people from the bondage and condemnation of sin.
Jews	Beginning in the period after the exile, the tribe of Judah comprised most of the families of Israel. As a result, the people became known as Jews. See Esther 2:5; 3:5–6.
Joy	An attitude leading to an emotion of cheer and contentment in God despite circumstances.
Judaism	The religious system of belief and lifestyle of the Jewish people.
Judaizers	A term used to describe those seeking to enforce upon Christians a Jewish lifestyle—particularly adherence to the Law of Moses and the rite of circumcision.
Justification	God's declaration of righteousness on an individual who has faith in Jesus Christ.
Law	A term widely used in the Bible to describe several important things: First, the term is used to describe the first five books of the Old Testament: Genesis, Exodus, Leviticus, and Deuteronomy. The Law is also used to describe the covenant between God and Israel established through Moses at Mount Sinai. Finally, it is also used in reference to the actual laws that were part of the Mosaic covenant, that is, the Ten Commandments.
Legalism	A mindset in which one seeks to live the Christian life based on certain human standards of conduct in an attempt to gain salvation or favor from God.
Mosaic Covenant	A conditional covenant made between God and Israel by the mediation of Moses at Mount Sinai. It is also known as the Sinai Covenant. Obedience to the covenant brought God's blessing and disobedience his discipline. The covenant was God's gracious guidance for life for Israel under his rule so that they would represent him properly among the nations.
Paul/Saul	A Jewish Pharisee who lived in the first century after Christ. He was the most formidable persecutor of the Christian church before becoming a leading proclaimer of the gospel.
pax romana	The peace that existed between nationalities within the Roman Empire. A system of peace brought about by the Empire by the force of the sword.
Pharisee	One of the major sects of Judaism of the first century. The Pharisees were particularly zealous in the keeping of the traditions and observances of Israel, especially the application of the law.
Redemption	A biblical concept used to describe the ransom paid to free something or someone for a price. With respect to salvation, it refers to the price paid by God to purchase, and so deliver mankind from its enslavement to sin.
Religio licita	A religion in the Roman Empire that was considered legal or "licit" by the government.
Sacrificial system	Name given to the group of ceremonial sacrifices ordained by God to Israel as a gracious means to cover the guilt and punishment for their sins. The sacrificial system included different types of offerings to God. They are described in detail primarily in Leviticus 1–7.
Sadducees	An aristocratic Jewish group of social, political, and religious influence who became responsible for maintaining the Jerusalem Temple during the times of the New Testament. This Jewish sect was characterized by their rationalism.
Salvation	Deliverance from the presence, power, and penalty of sin unto eternal life with God.
Sanctification	The process by which a Christian progresses in holiness by the operation of the Holy Spirit in his or her life. In this sense, sanctification is the work of God making a person righteous so that he or she can be in reality what he or she already is legally and positionally (justified). Sanctification is therefore the present, continuous aspect of Christian salvation.

Term	Definition
Sin	Any action, thought or intention that departs from the will of God as expressed in the Bible. The word is also used to describe the general state of moral and physical corruption of all of mankind and creation in general as the result of Adam's disobedience.
Timothy	A half-Jewish convert, disciple, and the missionary traveling companion of the apostle Paul. He was originally from the city of Lystra in Asia Minor. The Bible includes two letters addressed to him by Paul.
Trinity	The Christian doctrine of the Trinity teaches that the one true God exists in three distinct Persons—Father, Son, and Holy Spirit. Each distinct Person of the Godhead has distinct roles in the plan of salvation, but they are all co-equal.
Via Apia	One of the earliest and strategically most important Roman roads of the Empire. It connected Rome to Brindisi, Apulia, in southeast Italy.
Via Egnatia	One of the most important roads in the Roman Empire. Constructed by the Romans in the 2nd century BC. It crossed the Roman provinces of Illyricum, Macedonia, and Thrace, running through territory that is now part of modern Albania, the Republic of Macedonia, Greece, and European Turkey.
Walk	Idiom used in the Bible for how an individual lives or behaves in life. A particular lifestyle is thus described as a walk of life.
Yahweh	The covenant name of the one true God, the God of Israel. It could be translated simply, "I AM" or "I AM WHO I AM."

Tables and Charts

Scope of Salvation

Justification	Sanctification	Glorification
Declared saved	Being saved	Saved
Past tense of salvation	Present tense of salvation	Future tense of salvation
Freed from the penalty of sin	Being freed from the power of sin	Free from the presence of sin
Eternal life with God secured	Eternal life with God secured at justification	Experiencing eternal life with God because of justification
Romans 3:24; 5:1–2; 6:23 Ephesians 2:5, 8 Titus 3:5	Romans 5:9–10; 8 1 Corinthians 5:5 Galatians 5:16–26	Romans 8:30 1 Corinthians 15:42–44 1 Corinthians 15:51–53

Common Jewish Sects

	Pharisees	Sadducees	Essenes	Zealots	Herodians
Political group	Religious Conservatives	Political-Religious-Priestly liberals and conservatives	Religious ultra-conservatives	Political militants	Pro-Herodian kings and Pro-Roman
Authority	Law of Moses and its traditional oral interpretation	Law of Moses and priestly rights only	Law of Moses	Mixed: Law of Moses and Jewish right to national independence	Herodian monarchy
Social Class	Commoner	Aristocrats/Priestly Elite	Any	Any	Elite, Herod's extended family
Goal	Transform society	Rule society	Reject secularized society	Establish independent Jewish society	Maintain social and political power
Beliefs	Teach and apply the Law and interpretations, afterlife, resurrection, angelic beings, keep sacrifices and celebrate festivals of the Law	Uphold the Law, no afterlife, no resurrection, no angelic beings, maintain sacrifices of the Law at the Temple and manage the festivals	Belief in afterlife, abstinence, communal and simple living, purification rituals, rejection of established priesthood at the Temple	Mixed religious beliefs. Political and military focus.	Non-religious sect so beliefs unknown
Biblical Example	Saul/Paul	Caiaphas?	John the Baptist?	Simon the Zealot; Barabbas	?

For comments, corrections or suggestions, email us at
comments@SacraScript.org